LEARN SPANISH MADE EASY LEVEL 1

A Beginner's guide to basic grammar, vocabulary, verbs, sentence structure and traveling phrases.

ANTONIA REYES ORTEGA

© **Copyright 2022 Antonia Reyes Ortega - All rights reserved.**

The content contained within this book may not be reproduced, duplicated or transmitted without direct written permission from the author or the publisher.

Under no circumstances will any blame or legal responsibility be held against the publisher, or author, for any damages, reparation, or monetary loss due to the information contained within this book. Either directly or indirectly. You are responsible for your own choices, actions, and results.

Legal Notice:

This book is copyright protected. This book is only for personal use. You cannot amend, distribute, sell, use, quote or paraphrase any part, or the content within this book, without the consent of the author or publisher.

Disclaimer Notice:

Please note the information contained within this document is for educational and entertainment purposes only. All effort has been executed to present accurate, up to date, and reliable, complete information. No warranties of any kind are declared or implied. Readers acknowledge that the author is not engaging in the rendering of legal, financial, medical or professional advice. The content within this book has been derived from various sources. Please consult a licensed professional before attempting any techniques outlined in this book.

By reading this document, the reader agrees that under no circumstances is the author responsible for any losses, direct or indirect, which are incurred as a result of the use of the information contained within this document, including, but not limited to, — errors, omissions, or inaccuracies.

SPECIAL BONUS!

Want this Bonus Spanish Phrase Book for free?

Get **FREE**, unlimited access to it and all of my new books by joining the Fan Base!

  SCAN WITH YOUR CAMERA TO JOIN!

TABLE OF CONTENTS

INTRODUCTION 1

PART 1 – VOCABULARY AND SPANISH BASICS 5

CHAPTER 1: Spanish Phonetics 6

CHAPTER 2: Spanish Accent Marks 10

CHAPTER 3: Pronouns 14

CHAPTER 4: Common Nouns 20

CHAPTER 5: More Common Nouns 28

CHAPTER 6: Numbers 33

CHAPTER 7: Colors and Comparisons 38

CHAPTER 8: Adjectives 42

CHAPTER 9: Some Prepositions 48

CHAPTER 10: Days Of the Week and Months 53

CHAPTER 11: Shopping Vocabulary 59

CHAPTER 12: Food Vocabulary 62

CHAPTER 13: Holiday Vocabulary 66

CHAPTER 14: Compound Nouns 69

PART 2 – VERBS AND SENTENCE STRUCTURE 77

CHAPTER 1: Simple Present Tense and basic conjugations for "ar" "er" and "ir" verbs 78

CHAPTER 2: Common Verbs - Present Tense 81

CHAPTER 3: Some Irregular Verbs - Present Tense 89

CHAPTER 4: Simple Future 92

CHAPTER 5: Simple Past 94

CHAPTER 6: Imperfect Tense 97

CHAPTER 7: "Ser" and "Estar" 100

CHAPTER 8: "Por" and "Para" 102

CHAPTER 9: Basic Adverbs 104

CHAPTER 10: How to Build Sentences and Some Common Connectors 109

CHAPTER 11: Greetings and How to Introduce Yourself 116

CHAPTER 12: Telling Time 122

CHAPTER 13: The Weather 125

CHAPTER 14: Getting Directions 128

CHAPTER 15: Traveling in Spanish Speaking Countries 133

CONCULSION 137

INTRODUCTION

Welcome!

Learning languages is a tool that can help improve your quality of life or provide you with an incredible hobby and Spanish is an excellent choice, since it is the second most widely spoken language in the world after English.

Furthermore, Spanish is one of the languages derived from Latin (the languages that are part of this group are Portuguese, French, Italian, Romanian, Catalan, and Galician). So, if you love learning languages this is great news! Achieving a medium level of this language will mean that you know the grammatical structure of the Romance languages and that you will not have much difficulty when reading texts in these languages, since a high percentage of words have kept the same structure and although their pronunciation changes, they are very similar.

That is why I welcome you and congratulate you for having taken the first step to learning Spanish! From this moment I advise you to be clear about what your goals will be with this language so that you continue the path with them in mind. That way it will be easier not to give up and keep the will to practice.

In the following pages, we will cover essential topics such as the phonetics of the Spanish alphabet, numbers, basic greetings, how to formulate sentences, and vocabulary on various topics that you may want to keep handy for everyday use, like shopping and traveling.

My intention with this book is to help you take those first steps and guide you along the journey in your learning Spanish and clear up any doubts that you may have during it. This is why the first thing we will talk about is some of the main differences that exist between the two languages.

One of the biggest difference between English and Spanish is that Spanish has only five vowel sounds while English has more than fourteen (regional dialects may vary). This is the reason why Spanish speakers may find it difficult to differentiate between English words like "hop" and "hope".

There are many other differences between Spanish and English that are listed below so that you are prepared the moment they appear:

- Not only are there more letters in Spanish, but the consonants *h, j, ll, r, rr, v, x,* and *z* have very different pronunciations in the two languages. The consonant *ñ*, for example, does not exist in English; instead, the sound it represents is written with two letters, *ny*.
- In Spanish there are no verbal contractions such as "don't", "weren't", "isn't" etc.
- English suffixes and prefixes (*un-, over-, under-, -ly, -ness, -ful, -est*) are different from their Spanish counterparts.
- Another difference that you will come across regularly is that the names of nationalities, languages, days of the week, and months of the year are all capitalized in English, and in Spanish they are not.
- Question marks and exclamation marks are also a big difference between the two languages. In English they are placed only at the end of the sentence, but in Spanish, they are placed both at the beginning and the end of the sentence.
- The order of the words in the sentence varies significantly between English and Spanish.
- The use of adjectives is different between the two languages as well. In English, the adjective is always placed before the noun, because the purpose of the adjective is to modify or describe a noun. In Spanish, however, the adjective is usually placed after the noun. But there are some exceptions: if the adjective is a quantifier, it must be placed before the noun. For example: "the only room" should be written as *"el único cuarto"* (instead of *"el cuarto único"*).

The placement of the adjective can also change the meaning, we will see some examples in Chapter 5.

- In Spanish, there are two forms of the verb "to be". The first is "*ser*" and the second is "*estar*." Each of these is used differently.
- In English, negation can be much more complicated than it should be, since there is a wide variety of prefixes, such as "*not-*", "*un-*", "*dis-*", "*in-*" and many other negative words. That is why we must be careful to avoid using double negatives in our sentences. However, in Spanish, this is much easier, since its simplest form only asks us to put the word "no" before the verb and there are fewer prefixes to confuse you.

It may seem like too much if you still don't have a base of the language but don't worry because throughout this book we will return to each of these points!

PART 1
VOCABULARY AND SPANISH BASICS

CHAPTER 1:

SPANISH PHONETICS

"The alphabet." *"El alfabeto."*

A	B	C	D	E	F	G	H	I	J
a	be	ce	de	e	efe	ge	hache	i	jota
K	L	M	N	Ñ	O	P	Q	R	S
ka	ele	eme	ene	eñe	o	pe	koo	erre	ese
T	U	V	W	X	Y	Z			
te	u	uve	uve doble	equis	ye	zeta			

The alphabet of the Spanish language is made up of twenty-seven letters. They are only properly lettered the graphemes, that is to say, the simple graphic signs. In Spanish, in addition to the twenty-seven letters, there are five digraphs or two-letter combinations that are used to graphically represent the following sounds:

- *"Ch"* represents the sound / ch /: *"chocolate"* ("chocolate").
- *"Ll"* represents the sound / ll /: (or the sound /y/ depending on the speaker): *"lluvia"* ("rain").
- *"Gu"* represents the sound / g / before *"e"*, *"i"*: *"guepardo"* ("cheetah") *"guitarra"* ("guitar").
- *"Qu"* represents the sound / k / before *"e"*, *"i"*: *"queso"* ("cheese") *"quieto"* ("still").

- "*Rr*" represents the sound / rr / in intervocalic position: "*arroz*" ("rice"), "*perro*" ("dog").

The sounds for both letters "*B*" and "*V*" are slightly different in Spanish than English. The sounds are softened by native Spanish speakers. Native speakers do this by touching their lips together for a short moment and holding the sound for less time. This results in native speakers sometimes replacing "*v*" with "*b*" and vice versa. For instance, they may pronounce the word "*vaca*" ("cow") as / baca /.

Most often in Spanish, B and V are pronounced exactly the same.
For example: invierno (winter) is pronounced "inbierno".
However, if the B is followed by "l" or "r", it sounds more like a "B"
For example: blanco (white)

"C" has two sounds: like English "s" before *e* or *i*; like English "k" before *a, o, u*, or consonant:
"Cinema." "*Cine.*"
"House." "*Casa.*"

The "gu" letter grouping:
In the groups "gue", "gui" the *u* is mute (/ ge / / gi /); it is pronounced
"Handsome." "*Guapo.*"
"Water." "*Agua.*"

However, when the u has an umlaut (pronounced oomlout which is 2 dots above a letter) in the groups "gua" and "guo", it is pronounced:
"Shame." "*Vergüenza.*"
"Bilingual." "*Bilingüe.*"
"Penguin." "*Pingüino.*"

"H" is always silent (note that "*ch*" is a separate character):
"Hello." "*Hola.*"

"J" is like an English H, depending on the word. Sometimes pronounced as fricative (think Darth Vader):
"Son." "*Hijo.*"

"Eye." "*Ojo.*"

"*Ñ*" it's a consonant that exists only in the Spanish alphabet similar to the "*nio*" sound in English word "onion":

"Child." "*Niño.*"

"Spanish." "*Español.*"

"*Ll*", in most places, pronounced as Y.

"Chicken." "*Pollo.*"

"*P*" similar to English, but not aspirated as much.

"*Q*" I'ts always pronounced / k / and is found only in the groups "*que*", "*qui*". In these groups the *u* is mute; It is pronounced, on the other hand, in the groups "*cua*", "*cue*", "*cui*", "*cuo*":

"Four." "*Cuatro.*"
"Neck." "*Cuello.*"
"*Cuidado.*" "Care."
"Quota." "*Cuota.*"

In front of *a*, *o*, *u* and the consonants *l*, *r*, the letter "*g*" is pronounced like / g /:

"Goose." "*Ganso.*"
"Drop." "*Gota.*"
"Worm." "*Gusano.*"
"Big." "*Grande.*"
"Balloon." "*Globo.*"

"*R*" is pronounced with single flap except as initial sound, when it is always trilled.
"Fruit." "*Fruta.*" - trilled

"*W*" is rarely used in Spanish and usually only appears in words of foreign origin.
"*Wyoming.*"

"*Y*" is almost always like English Y sound:
"*Ya.*"

"*Z*" is almost always pronounced as English "*s*".

There are also two consonant groups like "*Gn*" where both consonant are pronounced separately:

"Magnific." "*Magnífico.*"
"Meaning." "*Significado.*"
"Dignity." "*Dignidad.*"

The other group is "*Sc*" and they are also pronounced separately:
"Pool." "*Piscina.*"
"Elevator." "*Ascensor.*"
"Scene." "*Escena.*"

CHAPTER 2:

SPANISH ACCENT MARKS

Spanish accents (tildes) are written only over the five vowels (*a, e, i, o, u*), and the accent is written from lower left to upper right: *á, é, í, ó, ú*.

There are two rules in Spanish that tell us where to put the stress within a word. This is important since stress can sometimes be the only way to distinguish between two words.

Rules for stressed words:

1. When words end in a vowel, the letter *n*, or the letter *s*, the stress is on the next to last syllable.

Examples:

- "All." "*Todo*" (***to***-*do*)
- "The exam." "*El examen*" (*e*-***xa***-*men*)
- "Young." "*Joven*." (***jo***-*ven*)
- "Monday." "*Lunes*." (***lu***-*nes*)
- "Intelligent." "*Inteligente*." (*in-te-li-****gen****-te*)

2. When words end in all other consonants (not *n* or *s*), the stress falls on the last syllable.

Examples:

- "To eat." "*Comer*." (*co-****mer***)

- "The city." "*La ciudad.*" (*ciu-**dad***)
- "The professor." "*El professor.*" (*pro-fe-**sor***)
- "The animal." "*El animal.*" (*a-ni-**mal***)

So if either of those two rules doesn't apply then we need to add an accent mark for emphasis. Let's look at one example in detail first:

- "The exams." "*Los exámenes.*"

This word ends in an "s", so the first rule says the stress should fall on the next to last syllable: e-xa-**me**-nes. But because this is an exception, it doesn't. The word maintains the same accent as its singular form, in what is now the third to last syllable, so we add an accent mark.

These are examples of Spanish words with accent marks that break the first rule:

- "The song." "*La canción.*" (*can-**cion***)
- "Too." "*También.*" (*tam-**bien***)
- "English." "*Inglés.*" (*in-**gles***)
- "Fast." "*Rápido.*" (***ra**-pi-do*)
- "Never." "*Jamás.*" (*ja-**mas***)

As you may have seen, none of the accents falls on the penultimate (this means second to last) syllable, as it normally would.

Here are a few examples of words that defy the second rule:

- "The grass." "*El césped.*" (***ces**-ped*)
- "The tree." "*El árbol.*" (***ar**-bol*)
- "Weak." "*Débil.*" (***de**-bil*)

The above words have something in common, they end in a consonant (not *n* or *s*), but their accent does not fall on the final syllable.

In Spanish, accent marks also serve to distinguish between words that are pronounced and written the same but have different meanings, these are called homonyms.

Here are some examples of common Spanish homonyms:

- "*El*" (masculine article) with the accent mark becomes "*él*" (he).
- "*Si*" (if) with the accent mark becomes "*sí*" (yes).
- "*Tu*" (your) with the accent mark becomes "*tú*" (you).
- "*Te*" (object: you) with the accent mark becomes "*té*" (tea).
- "*Mas*" (but) with the accent mark becomes "más" (more).

Spanish accents are also found on all inquisitive words when used in a question, indirect question or embedded question.

- "Who?" "*¿Quién?*"
- "What?" "*¿Qué?*"
- "Where?" "*¿Dónde?*"
- "How?" "*¿Cómo?*"
- "Why?" "*¿Por qué?*"
- "How much / many?" "*¿Cuánto?*"

Regular questions in Spanish are pretty basic and easy to spot, even so, let's take a look at some of these words in detail embedded in their corresponding examples.

When the word "*cómo*" (with accent) is used as "how", it carries an accent no matter where it falls in the sentence. (Without the accent, "*como*" means "like" or "as".)

- "*How is your mother?*" "*¿Cómo está tu madre?*"
- "*I don't understand how he does it.*" "*No entiendo cómo lo hace.*"

At the same time, when "*qué*" means an interrogative "what," it must carry an accent:

- "I don't know what to do." "*No sé qué hacer.*"

Whenever the word "*cuánto*" means "how much/many," it carries an accent:

- "I don't know how many there are." "*No sé cuántos hay.*"

There is no accent when these words are used in a question or an indirect question, but rather as a preposition or conjuuntion. Here are four example sentences of this situation:

- "You are like your father." "*Eres como tu padre.*"
- "I don't work when I'm sick." "*No trabajo cuando estoy enferma.*"
- "Juan says he is going to do it today." "Juan dice que lo va a hacer hoy".

CHAPTER 3:

PRONOUNS

A pronoun is a word that takes the place of a noun. The most used pronouns are the personal ones, but there are others such as interrogative, possessive, demonstrative, relative, and indefinite pronouns.

1. Personal pronouns are characterized by referring to people or things in third person. In the same way as nouns, personal pronouns can have the function of being the subject of a verb or the object of a verb or preposition:

- "We like him, but he doesn't like us."

It is important to note that most pronouns have different subject and object forms:

Subject Pronouns

	Singular	Singular	Plural	Plural
First person	I	*Yo*	We	*Nosotros, nosotras*
Second person	You	*Tú / Usted*	You	*Ustedes*
Third person	He, she, it	*Él, ella*	They	*Ellos, ellas*

If you pay attention to the second and third person, you may notice that there is an accent on "*tú*" and "*él*" to avoid confusion with the articles "el" and possessive pronouns "*tu*" and "*el*".

When you are going to memorize verbs, it will be easier if you remember this.

*Note: *Tú* is less formal than *Usted,* both meaning "you".

2. Object Pronouns (Direct or Indirect)

a. Direct Object Pronouns – Direct object Pronouns replace direct object nouns.

	Singular	Singular	Plural	Plural
First person	Me	*Me*	Us	*Nos*
Second person	You	*Te*	You	*Los, las*
Third person	he, she, it, you	*lo, la*	You	*Los, las*

Notes about Direct Object Pronouns:

- they are placed before the verb in Spanish (in English they go after the verb)
  ex. 'I saw her in the store" "La vi en tienda"
- In Spain, lo is replaced by le when referring to people

b. Indirect Object Pronouns

	Singular	Singular	Plural	Plural
First person	Me	*Me*	Us	*Nos*
Second person	You	*Te*	You	*Les*
Third person	Him, her, it	*Le*	Them	*Les*

- "José writes me a letter." "*José me escribe una carta.*"
- "María writes you a letter." "*María te escribe una carta.*"
- "Pedro writes him a letter." "*Pedro le escribe una carta.*"

However, when addressing formally with "*usted*", the pronoun "*le*" will also be used. In such cases, you will be able to differentiate it by context.

3. Now, **interrogative pronouns** such as "which", "what", and "who" are meant to replace a noun that refers to a person, an animal, or a thing and whose identity is unknown.

Function	Person	Persona	Object	Objeto
Subject	Who?, Whom?	¿Quién?, ¿A quién?	What?, Which?, Which one(s)?	¿Qué?, ¿Cuál?, ¿Cuáles?
Direct complement	Who?, Whom?	¿Quién?, ¿A quién?	What?, Which?, Which one(s)?	¿Qué?, ¿Cuál?, ¿Cuáles?
Indirect compliment	Who?, Whom?	¿Quién?, ¿A quién?	What?, Which?, Which one(s)?	¿A qué?, ¿A cuál?, ¿A cuáles?

This pronouns are used in direct and indirect interrogative sentences and are always written with an accent to differentiate themselves from the relative ones "*que*", "*cual*", and "*quien*", covered later in this chapter.

4. On the other hand, when we talk about **possessive pronouns**, we should keep in mind that they agree with what they describe, not with the owner itself.

	Masculine singular	Feminine singular	Masculine plural	Feminine plural
Mine	*El mío*	*La mía*	*Los míos*	*Las mías*
Yours (belonging to "*tú*")	*El tuyo*	*La tuya*	*Los tuyos*	*Las tuyas*
His, hers, its, yours (belonging to "*usted*")	*El suyo*	*La suya*	*Los suyos*	*Las suyas*
Ours	*El nuestro*	*La nuestra*	*Los nuestros*	*Las nuestras*
Theirs, yours (belonging to "*ustedes*")	*El suyo*	*La suya*	*Los suyos*	*Las suyas*

Examples:

- "That pencil is mine." "*Ese lápiz es mío.*"
- "That bag is mine." "*Esa bolsa es <u>la</u> mía.*"

Now you may ask how do we know when to use the definite articles "*el*", "*la*", "*los*", and "*las*" or when not to use it? How do we know when to say "*es mío*" or "*es <u>el</u> mío*"?

Well, even if grammatically you don't really need to use it, putting the definite article helps to stress the ownership.

5. Demonstrative pronouns are words used to point out people or things within a sentence.

	Meaning	**Masculine**	**Feminine**	**Neuter**
Singular	This, this one; that, that one; that, that one (further away)	*Este, ese, aquel*	*Esta, esa, aquella*	*Esto, eso, aquello*
Plural	These, these ones; those, those ones; those, those ones (further away)	*Estos, esos, aquellos*	*Estas, esas, aquellas*	

Note: In the past demonstrative pronouns were alway written with accents. The Spanish language institution has now ruled that they are not necessary.

Examples:

- "That dog was bigger than <u>this</u> one." "*Aquel perro era más grande que <u>este</u>.*"
- "I want these rings and <u>those</u> ones." "*Quiero estos anillos y <u>esos</u>.*"
- "I really did love <u>that</u>." "*Me encantó <u>aquello</u>.*"

Remember that all demonstrative pronouns have to agree with the noun that they are replacing. Also, neuter pronouns like "*esto*" and "*aquello*" are meant to talk about things you don't recognize or ideas.

*Note: Demonstrative Adjectives are identical to demonstrative pronouns, they do however, function differently. They modify nouns and indicative proximity to the speaker and the person or thing being spoken about. They are placed before the noun. See Chapter 8 on Adjectives for more about these adjectives.

6. A **relative pronoun** is a word that is responsible for introducing information about the person or thing that is being spoken about. They can also add more information about someone or something.

	Meaning	Masculine	Feminine
Singular	Who, that, whom	*Que, El que, quien*	*Que, La que, quien*
Plural	Who, that, whom	*Que, Los que, quienes*	*Que, Las que, quienes*

Example:

- "Manuel, who is a dedicated student, wants to be the student body president." "*Manuel, el que es un estudiante dedicado, quiere ser el presidente del cuerpo estudiantil.*"
- "The mall, the one which was built in 1950, is going to be closed." "*El centro comercial, que fue construido en 1950, va a ser clausurado.*"

As you may see, the words "which" and "that" are used to talk about things such as "*que*" in Spanish:

- "The movie that/which won the festival." "*La película que ganó el festival.*"
- "The book that/which I bought." "*El libro que compré.*"

One difference between the two languages is that in English we can leave out "*which*" and "*that*" but in Spanish you can't leave out "*que*".

Example:

- "The car (which) she wants to buy." "*El auto que ella quiere comprar.*"

7. Indefinite pronouns are used to talk in general about people or things without clarifying what or who they are. This group is made up of words such as "everything", "nothing", "nobody", etc.

"Everything / All." "*Todo.*"
"Nothing / Anything." "*Nada.*"
"Nobody / Anybody." "*Nadie.*"
"Something / Anything." "*Algo.*"
"Somebody / Anybody." "*Alguien.*"
"Some." "*Algunos.*"
"None / Any." "*Ninguno.*"
"Anybody / Any." "*Cualquiera.*"
"Much / Many." "*Mucho.*"
"Little / Few." "*Poco.*"
"Another one / Other." "*Otro.*"
"Each (one)." "*Cada uno.*"
"So much / So many." "*Tanto.*"
"Several." "*Varios.*"

Examples:

- "He has something for you." "*Él tiene algo para ti.*"
- "I didn't see anything." "*No vi nada.*"
- "There is none left." "*No queda ninguno.*"
- "I gave each one a sheet." "*Le di una hoja a cada uno.*"

note: "Todo" (everything) is followed by "lo que"

ex. "She is selling everything she has" "*Ella vende todo lo que tienne.*"

CHAPTER 4:

COMMON NOUNS

Family

Family is the most important part of life in Spanish-speaking countries and cultures. Family members are usually topics of everyday discussions. People from Spanish cultures tend to rely on their immediate family in good times and in less fortunate times as well.

Let's take a look at the immediate family. This is the most common vocabulary that you will probably hear and use the most when talking about family:

"The dad." "*El papá.*"
"The mom." "*La mamá.*"
"The mother." "*La madre.*"
"The father." "*El padre.*"
"The son." "*El hijo.*"
"The daughter." "*La hija.*"
"The brother." "*El hermano.*"
"The sister." "*La hermana.*"
"The siblings." "*Los hermanos.*"
"The parents." "*Los padres.*"

One difference that we find between English and Spanish is the existence of the word "siblings" to encompass brothers and sisters, which in Spanish does not exist since the masculine plural encompasses both. Also "Los padres" includes both mother and father.

In English there is only one definite article, "the". In Spanish, there are four definite articles to choose from: "*el*", "*la*", "*los*" and "*las*". In order to know which one to choose, you must take into account which is the noun that follows.

- "*El*" comes before masculine singular nouns.
- "*La*" comes before feminine singular nouns.
- When referring to a plural word that is masculine, "*los*" is used, whereas "*las*" comes before feminine plural words.

The extended family and the extended family are just as important as the nuclear one, so it may be useful to have a solid understanding of this topic's vocabulary:

"The relatives." "*Los parientes.*"
"The grandfather." "*El abuelo.*"
"The grandmother." "*La abuela.*"
"The grandson." "*El nieto.*"
"The granddaughter." "*La nieta.*"
"The uncle." "*El tío.*"
"The aunt." "*La tía.*"
"The nephew." "*El sobrino.*"
"The niece." "*La sobrina.*"
"The father in law." "*El suegro.*"
"The mother in law." "*La suegra.*"
"The son in law." "*El yerno.*"
"The daughter in law." "*La nuera.*"

Body Parts

As important as the family is, the individual person is equally important. Have you ever wondered what to call a part of your body? Let's take a look at all the parts of the body in Spanish or "*las partes del cuerpo*" so you can talk about these from head to toe!

"The head." "*La cabeza.*"

"The hair." "*El pelo.*"

"*Pelo*" is the most literal translation for "hair." However, "*pelo*" refers to any kind of body hair, there are more specific words like "*cabello*" that only refer only to the hair on a person's head.

"The ears." "*Las orejas.*"

While the Spanish word for the inner ear is "*el oído*", the external ear (what you are able to see) is called "*la oreja*".

"The face." "*La cara.*"

There are two different words for saying face in Spanish: "*la cara*" and "el rostro". While "*cara*" is usually used to talk about the physical part of the body, "*rostro*" is used to refer to the person's expression.

"The forehead." "*La frente.*"

"The eyes." "*Los ojos.*" (singular form: "The eye." "*El ojo.*")

"The eyebrows." "*Las cejas.*" (singular form: "The eyebrow." "*La ceja.*")

"The eyelashes." "*Las pestañas.*" (singular form: "The eyelash." "*La pestaña.*")

"The cheeks." "*Las mejillas.*" (singular form: "The cheek." "*La mejilla.*")

"The nose." "*La nariz.*"

"The mouth." "*La boca.*"

"The arms." "*Los brazos.*" (singular form: "The arm." "*El brazo.*")

"The elbows." "*Los codos.*" (singular form: "The elbow." "*El codo.*")

"The hands." "*Las manos.*" (singular form: "The hand." "*La mano.*")

"The legs." "*Las piernas.*" (singular form: "The leg." "*La pierna.*")

"The feet." "*Los pies.*" (singular form: "The foot." "*El pie*")

The names of body parts are used similarly in both Spanish and English, but with one main difference: the Spanish names of parts of the body are often preceded by the definite article ("*el*", "*la*", "*los*" or "*las*", meaning "the") instead of a possessive adjective (such as mi for "my" and tu for "your"). The possessive adjective is used only when it is unclear whose body part is being referring to.

Example:

- "Open your eyes!" "*¡Abre los ojos!*"
- "Shut your mouth!" "*¡Cierra la boca!*"
- "He bowed his head to pray." "*Inclinó la cabeza para rezar.*"

The possessive adjective is used when needed to avoid ambiguity:

- "I love your hair." "*Me encanta tu cabello.*"
- "I waved my hand." "*Agité mi mano.*"

Food

One of the best things to do while in Latin America or Spain is to eat!

These are some of the most general vocabulary words related to eating that you may hear or want to use while eating in a Spanish-speaking country:

"The food." "*La comida.*"
"The restaurant." "*El restaurante.*"
"The glass." "*El vaso.*"
"The spoon." "*La cuchara.*"
"The fork." "*El tenedor.*"
"The knife." "*El cuchillo.*"
"The dessert." "*El postre.*"
"The chicken." "*El pollo.*"
"The egg." "*El huevo.*"
"The apple." "*La manzana.*"
"The orange." "*La naranja.*"
"The pizza." "*La pizza.*"

You may have noticed that not all words start with the same article. Each Spanish noun has a gender indicated by the articles: *el* and *la* (masculine and feminine singular) or their plural forms *los* (masculine) and *las* (feminine).

To determine if a noun is feminine or masculine there are a few helpful general rules.

Most masculine nouns end in "o". An "o" ending usually indicates that a person or animal is male or that an item, place, etc. is grammatically masculine.

Examples:

"The son." "*El hijo.*"
"The book." "*El libro.*"
"The dog." "*El perro.*"
"The money." "*El dinero.*"
"The chicken." "*El pollo.*"

Exception: There are masculine nouns that don't end in "o". These words end in the following letters or letter combinations:

- an accented vowel (*á, é, í, ó, ú*)
- a consonant other than *d, z*
- *–ma*
- *e*

Examples:

1. "The hummingbird." "*El colibrí.*"
   This word, "*colibrí*" ends with an accented vowel and it's a masculine noun.

2. "The language." "*El idioma.*"
   The last syllable of this word is *-ma* and it's also a masculine noun.

3. "The tree." "*El árbol.*"
   This word ends with the consonant "*l*".

4. "The restaurant." "*El restaurante.*" or "The dessert." "*El postre.*"
   The words "*restaurante*" and "*postre*" end in "*e*".

More exceptions:

Not all the words that end in -*ma* are masculine. There are also cases like "*forma*", which means "form" and is feminine. And there are also many everyday words ending in *e* that are feminine, so these two rules must be taken carefully.

Most feminine nouns end in *a*. Usually a noun ending in an "*a*" indicates that the noun is female or grammatically feminine.

Examples:

"The daughter." "*La hija.*"
"The guitar." "*La guitarra.*"
"The spoon." "*La cuchara.*"
"The cow." "*La vaca.*"
"The apple." "*La manzana.*"

But there are also feminine nouns that don't end in "*a*" which usually end in *d*, *z*, or -*ión*.

Examples:

1. "The happiness." "*La felicidad.*" or "The health." "*La salud.*"
   These words end in *d*.

2. "The peace." "*La paz.*"
   This word ends in *z*.

3. "The song." "*La canción.*" or "The emotion." "*La emoción.*"
   The last syllable of these words is -*ión* and they are also feminine nouns.

Some exceptions for these rules like "*el día*" which means "the day" and ends with "*a*" and "*el pez*" which means "the fish" and ends with "*z*".

Other examples of this exception are:

"The host." "*El huésped.*"
"The map." "*El mapa.*"
"The grass." "*El césped.*"
"The pencil." "*El lápiz.*"

Plural nouns

Generally, the rule for Spanish plural nouns is that they almost always end in -s or -es. So let's take a look at the rules, and exceptions, that you need to know to pluralize Spanish nouns:

First, we have the nouns that end in a vowel. The rule for these cases states that singular nouns which end in an unstressed vowel (*a, e, i, o, u*) or a stressed vowel (*á, é* or *ó*), just need to add -s at the end to make it plural.

Examples:

"The brother." "*El hermano.*" turns into "The brothers." "*Los hermanos.*"
"The granddaughter." "*La nieta.*" turns into "The granddaughters." "*Las nietas.*"
"The orange." "*La naranja.*" turns into "The oranges." "*Las naranjas.*"
"The glass." "*El vaso.*" turns into "The glasses." "*Los vasos.*"

In the case of the remaining stressed vowels there is another option. If a singular noun ends in *í* or *ú*, you have to add -s or -es to pluralize the word. Both are correct but the -es plural form is considered to be a little more elegant.

As an example of this we have "the taboo", "*el tabú.*" which turns into "the taboos." and the Spanish form can be "*los tabús*" or "*los tabúes*"

Exceptions to it are the plurals of **loanwords** (words that Spanish adopted from foreign languages) that end in *í* or *ú*, which you obtain by adding -s to the end of words like "the menu" "*el menú*" to turn them into "the menus", "*los menús*".

Now let's learn about nouns that end in a consonant:

The rule states that you have to add -es at the end of singular nouns that end in a vowel plus *y* or the consonants *d, j, l, n, r, s, x, z,* or *ch*.

Examples:

"The king." "*El rey.*" turns into "The kings." "*Los reyes.*"
"The barrel." "*El barril.*" turns into "The barrels." "*Los barriles.*"
"The color." "*El color.*" turns into "The colors." "*Los colores.*"

"The button." "*El botón.*" turns into "The buttons." "*Los botones.*"

"The age." "*La edad.*" turns into "The ages." "*Las edades.*"

"The light." "*La luz.*" turns into "The lights." "*Las luces.*"

Something to keep in mind is that in the case of singular nouns which end in *z*, you will have to change the *z* to a *c* before adding *-es*.

Singular nouns that end in a consonant cluster (more than one consonant together) or a vowel plus a consonant other than *d, j, l, n, r, s, x, z,* or *ch*, are turned into a plural by adding –s at the end. An example of this is "the iceberg", "*el iceberg*" whose plural form remains the same in Spanish "the icebergs", "*los icebergs*".

But there are a few exceptions to the above rule like "the club", "*el club*" that becomes "the clubs", "*los clubes*".

CHAPTER 5:

MORE COMMON NOUNS

Since all the vocabulary related to **the house** in Spanish is really important in everyday conversations, we will learn in this lesson about the rooms and parts of the house in Spanish, and we will see how these words could be used in real situations.

"The bedroom." "*El dormitorio.*"
"The bathroom." "*El cuarto de baño.*"
"The kitchen." "*La cocina.*"
"The living room." "*La sala de estar.*"
"The hallway." " *El pasillo.*"
"The garden." "*El jardín.*"
"The basement." "*El sótano.*"
"The window." "*La ventana.*"
"The door." "*La puerta.*"

The verb "*tener*", means "to have", and we will see that it is very useful to talk about the parts of the house in Spanish, especially to say what objects a room has.
We also can use the adjective pronouns "*este*" and "*esta*" in sentences like:

- "This house has two bathrooms." "*Esta casa tiene dos cuartos de baño.*" (we use the adjective pronoun "*esta*" because it goes before the word "casa" which is feminine).

- "<u>This</u> bedroom has a window." "<u>Este</u> *dormitorio tiene una ventana.*" (we use the adjective pronoun "*este*" because it goes before the word "*dormitorio*" which is masculine).

Now that you know the house, you will need something to wear to go out. If you are shopping in a Spanish-speaking country on a holiday or visit, you will need to know some vocabulary.

The general word for "clothing" is "*la ropa*". It can refer to clothing in general or a specific article of clothing. Types of clothing for certain occasions include:

"*ropa deportiva*" or "*ropa sport*" (sportswear),
"traje de baño" (swim suit)
"*ropa informal*" (casual clothing),
"*ropa formal*" (formalwear) and
"*ropa para dormir*" (sleeping clothes)

Let's check out this list of clothing vocabulary:

"The t-shirt." "*La camiseta.*"
"The shirt." "*La camisa.*"
"The blouse." "*La blusa.*"
"The dress." "*El vestido.*"
"The sweatshirt." "*La sudadera.*"
"The sweater." "*El suéter.*" (or "*El jersey.*")
"The pants." "*El pantalón.*"
"The jeans." "*Los vaqueros.*" (or "*Los jeans.*")
"The skirt." "*La falda.*"
"The sneakers." "*Las zapatillas.*"
"The shoes." "*Los zapatos.*"
"The sandals." "*Las sandalias.*"
"The purse." "*El bolso.*"
"The tie." "*La corbata.*"
"The suit." "*El traje.*"

"The bikini." "*El biquini.*"
"The ring." "*El anillo.*"
"The earring." "*El arete.*"
"The necklace." "*El collar.*"
"The bracelet." "*La pulsera.*"
"The scarf." "*La bufanda.*"
"The cap." "*La gorra.*"
"The hat." "*El sombrero.*"
"The coat." "*El abrigo.*"
"The vest." "*El chaleco.*"
"The handkerchief." "*El pañuelo.*"
"The raincoat." "*El impermeable.*"

You can usually use "*ponerse*" to describe putting on clothing:

- "She put on the sweater without buttoning it." "Ella *se puso el jersey sin abotonarlo.*"

"*Sacarse*" and "*quitarse*" are usually used when describing the removal of clothes:

- "When she gets home, she takes off her coat." "*Cuando ella llega a casa, se quita el abrigo.*"
- "Ricardo wore a suit in the presentation and then he took off the jacket." "*Ricardo usó un traje en la presentación y luego se sacó el chaqueta.*"

The last verb related to clothing that we will see is "*cambiarse*", which is the verb of choice for changing possessions including clothing:

- "Your clothes smell bad, you must change them." "*Tu ropa huele mal, debes cambiarla.*"

The next thing we are going to talk about are **professions** in Spanish, so prepare yourself to see how to write and pronounce some of the most common occupations out there.

When asking someone what they do for employment you could say: "What do you do?" "*¿A qué te dedicas?*"

Spanish **profession nouns** change according to the gender of the person they refer to.

- "The banker."
  "El banquero." (masculine)
  "La banquera." (feminine)

- "The teacher."
  "El profesor." (masculine)
  "La profesora." (feminine)

- "The engineer."
  "El ingeniero." (masculine)
  "La ingeniera." (feminine)

- "The writer."
  "El escritor." (masculine)
  "La escritora." (feminine)

As we saw before, all nouns that end with "*o*" end with the letter "*a*" in its feminine form.

But there are also some nouns that end in *-ista*, *-ia* and *-e*, that stay the same for both male and female:

- "The dentist."
  "El dentista." (masculine)
  "La dentista." (feminine)

- "The police."
  "El policia." (masculine)
  "La policia." (feminine)

- "The student."

"El estudiante." (masculine)

"La estudiante." (feminine)

Let's look at the following examples of an everyday conversation:

1. **Q:** "What do you do, Paula?" *"¿A qué te dedicas, Paula?"*
   A: "Well, I'm a writer." *"Bueno, yo soy escritora."*

2. **Q:** "Hey, and what do you do (for a living)?" *"Oye, y ¿en qué trabajas?"*
   A: "I'm working currently at an Italian restaurant." *"Estoy trabajando actualmente en un restaurante italiano."*

3. **Q:** "I'm a banker, what about you?" *"Soy un banquero, ¿qué hay de ti?"*
   A: "I am a Spanish teacher." *"Yo soy profesor de español."*

CHAPTER 6:

NUMBERS

As in any other language, numbers are a great start for beginners: they always appear within everyday conversations, and it's really easy to get the hang of them. So you don't need to worry, because the Spanish cardinal number system is quite simple! Let's start, step by step, with the numbers 1 to 100 in Spanish:

0. "Zero." "*Cero.*"
1. "One." "*Uno.*"
2. "Two." "*Dos.*"
3. "Three." "*Tres.*"
4. "Four." "*Cuatro.*"
5. "Five." "*Cinco.*"
6. "Six." "*Seis.*"
7. "Seven." "*Siete.*"
8. "Eight." "*Ocho.*"
9. "Nine." "*Nueve.*"
10. **"Ten." "*Diez.*"**
11. "Eleven." "*Once.*"
12. "Twelve." "*Doce.*"
13. "Thirteen." "*Trece.*"
14. "Fourteen." "*Catorce.*"
15. "Fifteen." "*Quince.*"

To make numbers 16 to 19 you only need to add the to the prefix *dieci-* to the corresponding number (6 to 9):

16. "Sixteen." *"Dieciséis."*
17. "Seventeen." *"Diecisiete."*
18. "Eighteen." *"Dieciocho."*
19. "Nineteen." *"Diecinueve."*
20. "Twenty." *"Veinte."*

Numbers 21 to 29 are formed by adding the prefix *veinti-* to the corresponding number (1 to 9). Also you may have noticed that spelling rules indicate that *"veintidós"*, *"veintitrés"* and *"veintiséis"* have an accent mark, this was discussed in Chapter 2.

21. "Twenty-one." *"Veintiuno."*
22. "Twenty-two." *"Veintidós."*
23. "Twenty-three." *"Veintitrés."*
24. "Twenty-four." *"Veinticuatro."*
25. "Twenty-five." *"Veinticinco."*
26. "Twenty-six." *"Veintiséis."*
27. "Twenty-seven." *"Veintisiete."*
28. "Twenty-eight." *"Veintiocho."*
29. "Twenty-nine." *"Veintinueve."*
30. "Thirty." *"Treinta."*

After the number 30, we have a formula that is repeated for all the numbers between tens: "ten + *y* + unit". The letter *y* is the conjunction equivalent to "and" in Spanish. So the rest of the numbers will be written in the following way:

31. "Thirty-one." *"Treinta y uno."*
32. "Thirty-two." *"Treinta y dos."*
33. "Thirty-three." *"Treinta y tres."*
34. "Thirty-four." *"Treinta y cuatro."*
35. "Thirty-five." *"Treinta y cinco."*

36. "Thirty-six." *"Treinta y seis."*
37. "Thirty-seven." *"Treinta y siete."*
38. "Thirty-eight." *"Treinta y ocho."*
39. "Thirty-nine." *"Treinta y nueve."*

40. **"Forty." *"Cuarenta."***
41. "Forty-one." *"Cuarenta y uno."*
42. "Forty-two." *"Cuarenta y dos."*
43. "Forty-three." *"Cuarenta y tres."*
44. "Forty-four." *"Cuarenta y cuatro."*
45. "Forty-five." *"Cuarenta y cinco."*
46. "Forty-six." *"Cuarenta y seis."*
47. "Forty-seven." *"Cuarenta y siete."*
48. "Forty-eight." *"Cuarenta y ocho."*
49. "Forty-nine." *"Cuarenta y nueve."*

50. **"Fifty." *"Cincuenta."***
51. "Fifty-one." *"Cincuenta y uno."*
52. "Fifty-two." *"Cincuenta y dos."*
53. "Fifty-three." *"Cincuenta y tres."*
54. "Fifty-four." *"Cincuenta y cuatro."*
55. "Fifty-five." *"Cincuenta y cinco."*
56. "Fifty-six." *"Cincuenta y seis."*
57. "Fifty-seven." *"Cincuenta y siete."*
58. "Fifty-eight." *"Cincuenta y ocho."*
59. "Fifty-nine." *"Cincuenta y nueve."*

60. **"Sixty." *"Sesenta."***
61. "Sixty-one." *"Sesenta y uno."*
62. "Sixty-two." *"Sesenta y dos."*
63. "Sixty-three." *"Sesenta y tres."*
64. "Sixty-four." *"Sesenta y cuatro."*
65. "Sixty-five." *"Sesenta y cinco."*

66. "Sixty-six." *"Sesenta y seis."*
67. "Sixty-seven." *"Sesenta y siete."*
68. "Sixty-eight." *"Sesenta y ocho."*
69. "Sixty-nine." *"Sesenta y nueve."*
70. **"Seventy." *"Setenta."***
71. "Seventy-one." *"Setenta y uno."*
72. "Seventy-two." *"Setenta y dos."*
73. "Seventy-three." *"Setenta y tres."*
74. "Seventy-four." *"Setenta y cuatro."*
75. "Seventy-five." *"Setenta y cinco."*
76. "Seventy-six." *"Setenta y seis."*
77. "Seventy-seven." *"Setenta y siete."*
78. "Seventy-eight." *"Setenta y ocho."*
79. "Seventy-nine." *"Setenta y nueve."*
80. **"Eighty." *"Ochenta."***
81. "Eighty-one." *"Ochenta y uno."*
82. "Eighty-two." *"Ochenta y dos."*
83. "Eighty-three." *"Ochenta y tres."*
84. "Eighty-four." *"Ochenta y cuatro."*
85. "Eighty-five." *"Ochenta y cinco."*
86. "Eighty-six." *"Ochenta y seis."*
87. "Eighty-seven." *"Ochenta y siete."*
88. "Eighty-eight." *"Ochenta y ocho."*
89. "Eighty-nine." *"Ochenta y nueve."*
90. **"Ninety." *"Noventa."***
91. "Ninety-one." *"Noventa y uno."*
92. "Ninety-two." *"Noventa y dos."*
93. "Ninety-three." *"Noventa y tres."*
94. "Ninety-four." *"Noventa y cuatro."*
95. "Ninety-five." *"Noventa y cinco."*

96. "Ninety-six." "*Noventa y seis.*"
97. "Ninety-seven." "*Noventa y siete.*"
98. "Ninety-eight." "*Noventa y ocho.*"
99. "Ninety-nine." "*Noventa y nueve.*"
100. (One) "Hundred." "*Cien.*"

To write the hundreds from the number 200 to 900 (discounting 500, 700 and 900), you must write: the unit + *-cientos*.

200. "**Two hundred.**" "*Doscientos.*"
300. "**Three hundred.**" "*Trescientos.*"
400. "**Four hundred.**" "*Cuatrocientos.*"
500. "**Five hundred.**" "*Quinientos*
600. "**Six hundred.**" "*Seiscientos.*"
700. "**Seven hundred.**" "*Setecientos.*"
800. "**Eight hundred.**" "*Ochocientos.*"
900. "**Nine hundred.**" "*Novecientos.*"

1000. "**One thousand.**" "*Mil*"

CHAPTER 7:

COLORS AND COMPARISONS

The main colors in Spanish are:

"Black." "*Negro.*"
"Gray." "*Gris.*"
"White." "*Blanco.*"
"Yellow." "*Amarillo.*"
"Orange." "*Naranja.*"
"Brown." "*Marrón.*"
"Red." "*Rojo.*"
"Pink." "*Rosa.*"
"Purple." "*Púrpura.*"
"Blue." "*Azul.*"
"Green." "*Verde.*"

In daily use, colors have different forms. Like most of the Spanish adjectives, a color's gender must agree with the noun in gender and number.

As you may remember from Chapter 4, the colors maintain the same rule that nouns do: whether they end in *-o* or *-a*, will determine whether their form is masculine or feminine form as well as a singular or plural, so they must coincide with the noun.

The following examples show that there are four forms to refer to the color "*blanco*":

- "A white dog." "*Un perro blanco.*"

  In this case, "*blanco*" is in its masculine and singular form, just like the word it describes.

- "Some white dogs." "*Algunos perros blancos.*"

  Now we added an -*s* to "*blanco*" to convert it into the masculine plural form of the word: "*blancos*".

- "A white house." "*Una casa blanca.*"
- By replacing the final -*o* with an -*a* we got the feminine plural form of the word.
- "Some white houses." "*Unas casas blancas.*"
- Again, we got the feminine plural form by adding an -*s* at the end of the word.

When colors don't end in -*o* or -*a* (like "*verde*" and "*gris*"), there is no change between the masculine or feminine form. So you only need to add the -*s* or -*es* for its plural form.

Examples:

- "A green book." "*Un libro verde.*" (masculine singular form)
- "Some green books." "*Unos libros verdes.*" (masculine plural form)
- "A green light." "*Una luz verde.*" (feminine singular form)
- "Some green lights." "*Unas luces verdes.*" (feminine plural form)

When we describe colors, we can also mention tones, shades, and intensities with the following expressions:

"Bright." "*Brillante.*"
"Light." "*Claro.*"
"Dark." "*Oscuro.*"

"*Claro*" is the opposite of "*oscuro*" and "*brillante*" is a bright intense color that is easy to see. However, when we want to refer to "light blue", there is a Spanish specific word for it: "*celeste*".

Colors are a type of adjective that is used only after the noun. For example:

"Dark brown." "*Marrón oscuro.*"
"Light pink." "*Rosa claro.*"
"Bright red." "*Rojo brillante.*"

It is important to know, (except for a couple more exceptions) adjectives can be used both before and after nouns depending on the use.

Just as we can describe the color of things, comparing them is another tool that helps us define them in relation to something else. But is there a formula for making comparisons? There is!

Contrary to English, Spanish adjectives are not modified by adding suffixes (like *-er* and *-est*) for comparative purposes. In Spanish, adjectives will be accompanied by comparative structures to indicate the equality, inequality, or difference that exists between one or more people, objects, or ideas.

Regarding inequality, the comparison word will be accompanied by "más" (more) or "menos" (less). You can compare qualities (adjectives), ways of doing something (adverbs) or even nouns as in the following sentence:

- "The green box has <u>more</u> coins than the red one." "*La caja verde tiene <u>más</u> monedas que la roja.*"

Here are some common comparative structures:

- "*Más*" or "*Menos*" + adjective + "*que*"
  "Blue flowers are <u>more</u> <u>expensive</u> <u>than</u> white ones". "*Las flores azules son <u>más</u> <u>caras</u> <u>que</u> las blancas.*"
  "My arms are <u>more</u> <u>tanned</u> <u>than</u> yours." "*Mis brazos están <u>más</u> <u>bronceados</u> <u>que</u> los tuyos.*"

From these examples, we can see that the comparative particle "*que*" is the equivalent of "than" in English.

- "*Más*" or "*Menos*" + adverb + "*que*"
  "The plants were given compost to make them grow <u>faster</u>."
  "*A las plantas les pusieron abono para que crezcan <u>más</u> <u>rápido</u>.*"

Now, in this case we see that the particle "*que*" is not found because the second comparative term has not been mentioned:

- "Más" / "Menos" + noun + "que"

    "Family-sized products generate less waste per product unit."

    "*Los productos en tamaño familiar generan menos residuos por unidad de producto.*"

The same structure can be used with nouns. Here we see another difference between English and Spanish, according to traditional English rules, "fewer" is used for countable objects while "less" is used with singular mass nouns (i.e. sugar), this difference does not exist in Spanish. So Spanish-speakers will use "menos" for both countable and uncountable nouns.

The Spanish verb "*tener años*" means "to have years" (being a certain age), the expression "*tengo más años que mi primo*" ("I have more years than my cousin") is translated as "I am older than my cousin".

Examples (both are correct):

- "I am two years younger than you." "*Yo tengo dos años menos que tú.*"
- "I am two years younger than you." "*Yo soy dos años menor que tú.*"

In these examples, we can see (even if the position of the noun is different) that prepositional object pronouns like "*mí*" and "*ti*" can't be used in comparatives serving to compare two or more things as the second object of comparison (after "*que*").

CHAPTER 8:

ADJECTIVES

Since describing people, things, feelings, and situations is an essential part of speaking a language, it's important to have a good understanding of Spanish adjectives.

Spanish is a very descriptive language and therefore there are many possible adjectives available. Let's look at some common ones:

Appearance adjectives:

"Tall." "*Alto.*"
"Long." "*Largo.*"
"Short." "*Bajo.*"
"Young." "*Joven.*"
"Old." "*Viejo.*"
"Beautiful." "*Hermoso.*"
"Ugly." "*Feo.*"
"Handsome." "*Guapo.*"
"Fat." "*Gordo.*"
"Thin." "*Flaco.*"
"Strong." "*Fuerte.*"
"Weak." "*Débil.*"
"Pale." "*Pálido.*"

Examples:

- "Emilio is tall and handsome." "*Emilio es alto y guapo.*"
- "My grandmother is old and short." "*Mi abuela es vieja y baja.*"
- "My cousin is thin and pale, he looks like a vampire!" "*Mi primo es flaco y pálido, ¡se ve como un vampiro!*"
- "Ana has long hair." "*Ana tiene el pelo largo.*"

Other adjectives for hair are: "*rubio*" ("blond"), "*castaño*" ("brunnete"), "*pelirrojo*" ("redhead").

Personality adjectives:

"Sympathetic." "*Simpático.*"
"Intelligent." "*Inteligente.*"
"Fool." "*Tonto.*"
"Honest." "*Honesto.*"
"Generous." "*Generoso.*"
"Organized." "*Organizado.*"
"Lazy." "*Perezoso.*"
"Serious." "*Serio.*"
"Extroverted." "*Extrovertido.*"
"Introverted." "*Introvertido.*"
"Nice." "*Agradable.*"

Examples:

- "Florencia is organized and serious when she is at work." "*Florencia es organizada y seria cuando está en el trabajo.*"
- "Jorge is generous. He always gives expensive gifts." "*Jorge es generoso. Él siempre da regalos costosos.*"
- "Marta is honest and intelligent. She always tells the truth and has good grades." "*Marta es honesta e inteligente. Ella siempre dice la verdad y tiene buenas notas.*"

- "Damian is extroverted; he invited the whole school to his party." *"Damián es extrovertido; invitó a toda la escuela a su fiesta."*

Feelings and states:

"Sad." *"Triste."*
"Happy." *"Contento."*
"Angry." *"Enojado."*
"Scared." *"Asustado."*
"Embarrassed." *"Avergonzado."*
"Tired." *"Cansado."*

- "My sister is sad because she lost her favourite necklace." *"Mi hermana está triste porque perdió su collar favorito."*
- "I'm really tired; I spent the whole night working on my project." *"Estoy muy cansado. Pasé toda la noche trabajando en mi proyecto."*
- "My dad gets angry when my older sister has bad grades." *"Mi papa se enoja cuando mi hermana tiene malas calificaciones."*
- "Carlos saw the spider and now he's scared." *"Carlos vio la araña y ahora está asustado."*

Other adjectives:

"Cold." *"Frío."*
"Hot." *"Caliente."*
"Fast." *"Rápido."*
"Slow." *"Lento."*
"Clean." *"Limpio."*
"Dirty." *"Sucio."*
"Square." *"Cuadrado."*
"Round." *"Redondo."*
"Rectangular." *"Rectangular."*

The endings of Spanish adjectives must agree with the nouns they modify, both in gender and number. There are two types of adjectives:

1. The ones that end in -*o*.

   For adjectives ending in -*o* simply replace the -*o* with an -*a* when the noun is feminine, as well as add -*s* to pluralize. For example:

   - "The tired dog." "*El perro cansado.*" (here the adjective stays in the masculine singular form).
   - "The angry mom." "*La mamá enojada.*" (now we replaced the final -*o* of the adjective "*contento*" with an -*a* to convert it in the feminine singular form of the word).
   - "The long pencils." "*Los lápices largos.*" ("*largos*" is the masculine plural form of the word "*largo*").
   - "The red apples." "*Las manzanas rojas.*" ("*rojas*" is the feminine plural form of the word "*rojo*").

2. The ones that end in everything else.

   Adjectives may end in -*e* or in consonants and remain the same for both masculine and feminine nouns.

   To pluralize adjectives that end in an *e* add "*s*"

   For example:

   - "The intelligent sister." "*La hermana inteligente.*" ("*Inteligente*" even if the noun is feminine).
   - "The intelligent sisters." "*Las hermanas inteligentes*" (An -*s* was added at the end to pluralize the adjective).

   To pluralize adjectives that end in a consonant, add "-*es*".

   - "The grey wall." "*La pared gris.*" "The grey walls." "*Las paredes grises.*"

There is an exception, for the few adjectives that end in -*z*, such as "happy", "*feliz*", you just drop the -*z* and add –*ces* to obtain its plural form:

"The happy dogs." "*Los perros felices.*"

Adjectives in Spanish can be situated before or after the noun but there are differences in use:

1. An adjective that goes **after** the noun serves to distinguish the object (the noun) from the other objects.

    - "I don't like cold pizza." "*No me gusta la pizza fría.*" (We distinguish the pizza, specifically the cold one).
    - "I like fast cars." "*Me gustan los coches rápidos.*" (Distinction: he doesn't like slow ones).

2. An adjective that goes **before** the noun is used to highlight a characteristic of the object, but not to distinguish it.

    - "I like the small guitar." "*Me gusta la pequeña guitarra.*" (We distinguish the guitar itself).
    - "I don't like the big tree." "*No me gusta el gran árbol.*" (Distinction: the tree itself).

But be careful, like colors there are other adjectives that can **only** be **after** nouns:

- Colors: "*un libro... verde / azul / rojo / amarillo.*"
- Forms: "*una pizza... cuadrada / redonda / rectangular.*"
- States: "*un vaso... vacío / lleno / roto.*"

This rule can only be broken in the use of poetic language:

- "In the dark room only the green eyes of the woman shone." "*En el <u>oscuro</u> cuarto solo brillaban los <u>verdes</u> ojos de la mujer.*

Demonstrative adjectives are identical to demonstrative pronouns covered in Chapter 3.

	Meaning	Masculine	Feminine	Neuter
Singular	This, this one; that, that one; that, that one (further away)	*Este, ese, aquel*	*Esta, esa, aquella*	*Esto, eso, aquello*
Plural	These, these ones; those, those ones; those, those ones (further away)	*Estos, esos, aquellos*	*Estas, esas, aquellas*	

Demonstrative Adjectives, do however, function differently. They modify nouns and indicate proximity to the speaker and the person or thing being spoken about.

Este and its feminine plural forms refer to something close to the speaker.
Ese and its other forms refer to something further away from the speaker (ex. there).
Aquel, and its other forms, refer to something even further away (ex. over there).

Examples:

"Este chico habla mucho." "This boy talks a lot."
"Esas casas son muy caras." "Those houses are very expensive."
"A él, le gustan aquellas pinturas." "He likes those paintings." Meaning the paintings over there.

Now that you have an overview of adjectives in Spanish, you are now ready to describe everything you want to!

CHAPTER 9:

SOME PREPOSITIONS

Since prepositions are used before nouns and pronouns (like "the man", "the woman", "me") they show the relationship between the noun or pronoun and the rest of the sentence. In English, prepositions can be used before verb forms that end in *-ing* in English, but in Spanish, they're followed by the infinitive (the form of the verb ending in *-ar*, *-er*, or *-ir*):

- **"A"**

    When *a* is followed by "*el*", the two words merge to become "*al*".

    1. "*A*" can mean "to" when we are talking about places and destinations:

        - "I'm going to the cinema." "*Voy al cine.*" ("*cine*" has the masculine pronoun "*el*")
        - "I'm going to Madrid." "*Voy a Madrid.*"

    2. "*A*" can mean "to" with indirect objects:

        - "He gave it to María." "*Se lo dio a María.*"

    3. "*A*" can mean "to" when it comes after "*ir*" while talking about what someone is going to do:

        - "I'm going to see her tomorrow." "*Voy a verla mañana.*"

    4. "*A*" can mean "at" with times:

- "At five o'clock." "*A las cinco.*"

5. "*A*" can mean "at" with prices and rates:
   - "At 100 km per hour." "*A 100 km por hora.*"
   - "(at) two euros a kilo." "*A dos euros el kilo.*"

6. "*A*" can mean "at" with ages:
   - "At the age of 18." "*A los 18 años.*"

7. "*A*" can mean "onto":
   - "He fell onto the floor." "*Se cayó al suelo.*"

8. "*A*" can mean "into":
   - "To stick a photo into the album." "*Pegar una foto al álbum.*" ("*álbum*" has the masculine pronoun "*el*")

9. "*A*" is also used to talk about distance:
   - "(at a distance of) 11 km from here." "*A 11 km de aquí.*"

10. "*A*" can mean "from" after certain verbs:
    - "I bought it from my nephew." "*Se lo compré a mi sobrino.*"
    - "He was stealing money from his classmates." "*Les robaba dinero a sus compañeros de clase.*"

These are some extras. "*A*" can be used in set phrases as "*a veces*" "at times" and "*a menudo*" "often". Also, "*a*" can be used to talk about the conventional manner in which something is done:

- "In the English manner." "*A la inglesa.*"

Also you can't use "*a*" to mean "at" when talking about a building, city, or certain area where someone is. You will have to use "*en*" instead.

- **"*De*"**

Similar to the case of "*a*", when "*de*" is followed by "*el*", the two words merge to become "*del*".

1. *"De"* can mean "from":

    - "I'm from London." *"Soy de Londres."*
    - "A doctor from Valencia." *"Un médico de Valencia."*

2. *"De"* is also used with *"a"* to mean "from…" "to …"

    - "From morning to night." *"De la mañana a la noche."*

3. *"De"* can mean "of":

    - "The president of France." *"El presidente de Francia."*
    - "Two litres of water." *"Dos litros de agua."*

4. *"De"* can show who or what something belongs to:

    - "My father's hat." (literally: the hat of my father) *"El sombrero de mi padre."*

5. *"De"* can describe what something is made of, its content, or what it is used for:

    - "A lace dress." *"Un vestido de cordón."*
    - "A cup of tea." *"Una taza de té."*

6. *"De"* is used in comparisons when a number is mentioned:

    - "There were more than 20 types of food." *"Había más de 20 tipos de comida."*

    *Even if you normally would use *"que"* with *"más"* or *"menos"*, it is not used when there is a number involved.

7. *"De"* can mean "in" after superlatives (the most…, the biggest, the least…):

    - "The most beautiful city in the world." *"La ciudad más hermosa del mundo."* (*"mundo"* has the masculine pronoun *"el"*)

8. *"De"* is also used after certain adjectives and verbs:

    - "Pleased to see." *"Contento de ver."*
    - "It's difficult to understand." *"Es difícil de entender."*

9. *"De"* is often used in descriptions:

   - *"*The woman in the blue hat.*"* *"La mujer del sombrero azul."* (*"sombrero"* has the masculine pronoun *"el"*)
   - *"*A boy with green eyes.*"* *"Un chico de ojos verdes."*

- *"En"*

  1. *"En"* can mean *"in"* with places:

     - *"*In Mexico.*"* *"En México."*
     - *"*In bed.*"* *"En la cama."*
     - *"*In the cinema.*"* *"En el cine."*

  2. *"En"* can mean *"at"*:

     - *"*At home.*"* *"En casa."*
     - *"*At school.*"* *"En la escuela."*

  3. *"En"* can mean *"in"* with languages and in set phrases:

     - *"*It's written in English.*"* *"Está escrito en inglés."*
     - *"*In a low voice.*"* *"En voz baja."*

  4. *"En"* can mean *"on"*:

     - *"*Sitting on a chair.*"* *"Sentado en una silla."*
     - *"*There is one picture on the wall.*"* *"Hay un cuadro en la pared."*

  5. *"En"* can mean *"by"* with most methods of transport:

     - *"*By plane.*"* *"En avión."*
     - *"*By car.*"* *"En coche."*

  6. *"En"* can mean *"into"*:

     - *"*Let's go into the house.*"* *"Entremos en la casa."*

  7. *"En"* is also used after certain adjectives and verbs:

- "She is very good at geography." "*Es muy buena en geografía.*"

8. "*En*" can mean "in" when we are talking about months, years and seasons, and when something happened or how long something takes:

    - "In March." "*En Marzo.*"
    - "In 2020." "*En 2020.*"
    - "He was born in spring." "*Nació en primavera.*"

Here are two Spanish examples that have very different meanings. They both translate the same in English, so you may have to look for other contextual clues to understand exactly what is meant:

Example: "I'll do it in a week."

1. "*Lo haré dentro de una semana.*" (means that you'll do it within a week)
2. "*Lo haré en una semana.*" (means that you will do it in a week)

CHAPTER 10:

DAYS OF THE WEEK AND MONTHS

Days of the Week

Now let's learn seven important words that you'll use regularly when speaking Spanish. Here are "the days of the week"; "*los días de la semana*".

"Monday." "*lunes.*"
"Tuesday." "*martes.*"
"Wednesday." "*miércoles.*"
"Thursday." "*jueves.*"
"Friday." "*viernes.*"
"Saturday." "*sábado.*"
"Sunday." "*domingo.*"

Something to remember is the days of the week in Spanish are **not** capitalized:

- "I don't have class on Saturday." "*No tengo clase el sábado.*"
- "See you on Monday!" "*¡Nos vemos el lunes!*"

Also remember that not all the days of the week take the masculine article.

Most of the Spanish words for the days of the week originate from heavenly bodies, because of their Greco-Roman origins:

- "*Lunes*" was named for the moon or "*la luna*".
- "*Martes*" comes from Mars or "*Marte*".

- *"Miércoles"* was named for Mercury or *"Mercurio."*
- *"Jueves"* comes from Jupiter or *"Júpiter"*.
- *"Viernes"* was named for Venus (in Spanish it is written the same way).
- *"Sábado"* comes from *"sabat"* (Hebrew word for *rest*).
- *"Domingo"* was named for *"Dominus"* (Lord in Latin).

Similarly to English, the singular and plural forms of the days of the week which end in *"s"* stay the same in Spanish. You only need to change the article:

- "On Monday." *"El lunes."* (singular article).
- "On Mondays." *"Los lunes."* (plural article).

If the day ends in *"o"*, then add an *"s"*.

Months

It is important to know the twelve words for months in case you need to plan a trip, book a hotel, or just to describe what the date is. Here are the names of "the months" or *"los meses"*:

"January." *"enero."*
"February." *"febrero."*
"March." *"marzo."*
"April." *"abril."*
"May." *"mayo."*
"June." *"junio."*
"July." *"julio."*
"August." *"agosto."*
"September." *"septiembre."*
"October." *"octubre."*
"November." *"noviembre."*
"December." *"diciembre."*

In English the month can come before or after the day, but in Spanish, the month comes after the day.

Example:

In English we can say "Today is November fifth." or "Today is the fifth of November." and both are correct. But in Spanish we only can say "*Hoy es el cinco de noviembre.*"

In Spanish, the year usually comes after the day and the month, let's look at some different ways to write the entire date:

- "March 4" "*4 de Marzo*".
- "March 4, 2018" "*4 de Marzo de 2018*".
- "03/04/2018" "04/03/2018".
- "March fourth two thousand eighteen" "*cuatro de marzo de dos mil dieciocho*".

In Spanish you will write the date using "*de*" or "*del*" (this one is considered more formal) before the year.

- 4 de marzo de 2018
- 4 de marzo del 2018

In English **ordinal** numbers are used to describe the date, but in the Spanish language, **cardinal** numbers are normally used. While cardinal numbers are counting ones like "*uno*", "*dos*", and "*tres*", ordinal numbers are there to put things in order.

Let's take a moment to see the first ten ordinals which are used very often:

"First." "*Primero.*"
"Second." "*Segundo.*"
"Third." "*Tercero.*"
"Fourth." "*Cuarto.*"
"Fifth." "*Quinto.*"
"Sixth." "*Sexto.*"
"Seventh." "*Séptimo.*"
"Eight." "*Octavo.*"
"Ninth." "*Noveno.*"

"Tenth." "Décimo."

Spanish ordinal numbers go before the noun and have to agree with the gender and number of the noun they are describing:

- "The first paintings were beautiful." "*Las <u>primeras</u> pinturas eran hermosas.*"

One rule about the ordinals "*primero*" (first) and "*tercero*" (third) is that they drop the final 'o' before a masculine noun:

- "The first day of June." "*El primer día de Junio.*"

Now, you should keep in mind that ordinal numbers can be **simple** or **compound**. Whereas simple ordinals have their own form, compound ones are made by joining simple numbers. For example, we could write the ordinal "thirteenth" as a simple number "*treceavo*" or as a compound one "*décimo tercero*":

"Eleventh" can be "*onceavo*" or "*décimo primero*".
"Twelfth" can be "*doceavo*" or "*décimo segundo*".
"Thirteenth" can be "*treceavo*" or "*décimo tercero*".
"Fourteenth" can be "*catorceavo*" or "*décimo cuarto*".
"Fifteenth" can be "*quinceavo*" or "*décimo quinto*".
"Sixteenth" can be "*dieciseisavo*" or "*décimo sexto*".
"Seventeenth" can be "*diecisieteavo*" or "*décimo séptimo*".
"Eighteenth" can be "*dieciochoavo*" or "*décimo octavo*".
"Nineteenth" can be "*diecinueveavo*" or "*décimo noveno*".

"Twentieth." "*Vigésimo.*"

Remember, we also make use of ordinal numbers while talking about sovereign figures like kings and queens (popes too). In this case, the ordinals are placed after the noun they describe:

- "That's Pope John Paul the Second." "*Ese es el Papa, Juan Pablo Segundo.*"

Next, we will look at **the seasons**. So the first thing to keep in mind is how to say "season" in Spanish: while its singular form we say "*estación*", its plural form is "*estaciones*". The second thing is just a simple observation: all seasons except "spring" are masculine nouns (the three of them end with -*o*).

The names of the four seasons are:

"Summer." "Verano."

"Autumn." "Otoño."

"Winter." "Invierno."

"Spring." "Primavera."

Unlike the days of the week, the origin of the names of the seasons comes from Latin:

- "*Verano*" originates from "*veranum*", which in Latin could refer to either spring or summer.
- "*Otoño*" originates from "*autumnus*", which is the root of the English "autumn."
- "*Invierno*" originates from "*hibernum*", which is also the Latin root for "hibernate."
- "*Primavera*" is related to "*primera*" ("first") and "*ver*" ("to see"), because it is the time of year when it is possible to first see new life.

The equivalent of their adjectival form, such as "wintry" and "summery", is sometimes used: "*invernal*" ("wintry"), "*primaveral*" ("springlike"), "*veraniego*" ("summery"), and "*otoñal*" ("autumnal").

"*Verano*" also has a verb form, "*veranear*", which refers to how you spend the summer (vacation or holiday).

Technically, the seasons are considered to begin and end on the longest and shortest days of the year. We know that summer begins around June 21 in the Northern Hemisphere but in the Southern Hemisphere it starts around December 21.

However, practically speaking, summer can also be thought of as including the hottest months, generally June, July, and August in the Northern Hemisphere, but in the Southern Hemisphere the hottest months are December, January, and February.

To help make it clearer, in much of the tropics they refer to two locally recognized seasons:

- "Rainy season (or wet season)." "*La estación lluviosa.*"
- "Dry season." "*La estación seca.*"

Let's practice with some sentences:

- "Today is the third day of spring and I can see that the flowers have already begun to bloom." "*Hoy es el tercer día de primavera y puedo ver que las flores ya han comenzado a florecer.*"
- "On the third Saturday of every month my parents organize a party." "*El tercer sábado de cada mes mis padres organizan una fiesta.*"
- "In Latin America, Christmas is in summer and there is no snow." "*En Latinoamérica, la Navidad es en verano y no hay nieve.*"

CHAPTER 11:

SHOPPING VOCABULARY

If you are like most tourists, when you travel to other countries you will probably want to visit the local shops and markets to get some souvenirs so you can take them back with you. You might also want to pick up a few groceries or living necessities.

The first thing that usually comes to mind when we think about buying is probably money (what will it cost). That is why being able to ask for the price of things is vital if you want to make a purchase. Here are some words and phrases to help you talk about the cost in Spanish:

"The coin." "*La moneda.*"
"The money." "*El dinero.*"
"The bill." "*El billete.*"
"The change." "*El cambio.*"
"The credit card." "*La tarjeta de crédito.*"
"The debit card." "*La tarjeta de débito.*"
"The check." "*El cheque.*"
"The cash." "*El efectivo.*"
"The sale." "*La oferta.*"
"The shop." "*La tienda.*"
"Open." "*Abierto.*"
"Closed." "*Cerrado.*"

Now, here is a tip to remember the names of some kind of shops. A common suffix used with Spanish nouns, *-ería*, indicates where something is made or sold. You will come across the word most often as specialty store names, like *"librería"* for "library" and *"panadería"* for "bakery". Also, all these nouns are feminine.

- "Coffee shop." *"Cafetería."* (from *"café"*, "coffee")
- "Brewery." *"Cervezería."* (from *"cerveza"*, "beer")
- "Jewelry shop." *"Joyería."* (from *"joya"*, "jewel")
- "Toy shop." *"Juguetería."* (from *"juguete"*, "toy")
- "Bookstore." *"Librería."* (from *"libro"*, "book")
- "Bakery." *"Panadería."* (from *"pan"*, bread)
- "Produce store." *"Verdulería."* (from *"verdure"*, "vegetable")
- "Shoe store." *"Zapatería."* (from *"zapato"*, "shoe")

Other stores:

"Department store." *"Almacén."*
"Clothing store." *"Tienda de ropa."*
"Supermarket." *"Supermercado."*

Looking for a specific item? You might want to describe it to a store assistant to spreed things up. The more descriptive you are, the easier it will for them to help you.

- "Excuse me…" *"Disculpe…"*
- "I'm looking for…" *"Estoy buscando…"*
- "I'm only looking." *"Solo estoy mirando."*
- "Do you have... in other colors?" *"¿Tiene... en otros colores?"*
- "Do you have ... in other sizes?" *"¿Tiene… en otras tallas?"*
- "Good quality." *"De buena calidad."*
- "Poor quality." *"De mala calidad."*
- "Can I see that one?" *"¿Puedo ver ese?"*
- "Can I try it on?" *"¿Me lo puedo probar?"*
- "Which one would you recommend?" *"¿Cuál me recomendaría?"*

But don't spend all your money! Remember to budget, you might want to say:

- "How much does it cost?" "*¿Cuánto cuesta?*"
- "It is (very) expensive." "*Es (muy) caro.*"
- "It is (very) cheap." "*Es (muy) barato.*"

Here are also some phrases that you may need to say or understand when making a purchase:

- "Do you take credit cards?" "*¿Aceptan tarjetas de crédito?*"
- "How would you like to pay?" "*¿Cómo le gustaría pagar?*"
- "Please enter your PIN." "*Ingrese su PIN, por favor.*"
- "Please sign here." "*Firme aquí, por favor.*"
- "Can I get a refund?" "*¿Se aceptan devoluciones?*"
- "Can I have a bag?" "*¿Tiene una bolsa?*"

CHAPTER 12:

FOOD VOCABULARY

Food is an essential part of our lives, and it is important to have at least three big meals, so let's start at the beginning of our day: breakfast.

Breakfast and its content vary greatly depending on the country you are in, but still, let's take a look at the most common ingredients when making it.

"The coffee." "*El café.*"
"The tea." "*El té.*"
"The milk." "*La leche.*"
"The bread." "*El pan.*"
"The toast." "*La tostada.*"
"The bacon." "*El tocino.*"
"The cereals." "*Los cereales.*"
"The yoghurt." "*El yogur.*"
"The honey." "*La miel.*"
"The eggs." "*Los huevos.*"
The sausages." "*Las salchichas.*"
"The beans." "*Los frijoles.*"
"The cheese." "*El queso.*"
"The jam." "*La mermelada.*"
"The ham." "*El jamón.*"

Now, throughout our day, we probably want to incorporate carbohydrates, fruits, vegetables, and meats into our diet, so in the following list, we can expand our vocabulary about them!

"The meat." "*La carne.*"
"The lamb." "*El cordero.*"
"The chicken." "*El pollo.*"
"The fish." "*El pescado.*"
"The soup." "*La sopa.*"
"The rice." "*El arroz.*"
"The fruit." "*La fruta.*"
"The peach." "*El durazno.*"
"The watermelon." "*La sandía.*"
"The banana." "*El plátano.*"
"The grape." "*La uva.*"
"The pear." "*La pera.*"
"The strawberry." "*La fresa.*"
"The lemon." "*El limón.*"
"The lemonade." "*La limonada.*"
"The vegetables." "*Los vegetales.*"
"The carrot." "*La zanahoria.*"
"The broccoli." "*El broccoli.*"
"The ice cream." "*El helado.*"

When we talk about food, we enter a world full of new experiences, since, like new dishes to try, there are always new words to learn.

That is why in this section we will see a series of ingredients and common dishes in Spanish-speaking countries, as well as for instructions when following a recipe.

Starting with some of the flavors most typical of the Spanish-speaking Latin American countries, we can mention the following dishes:

- "*Chile relleno.*"

Stuffed peppers are a Guatemalan meal that consists of roasted chili peppers that are peeled, and the seeds removed and then stuffed. It is generally used with different meats and is served with rice.

- *"Asado criollo."*

    It is a typical Argentine barbecue in which you can cook various types of meat, including lamb, beef, and chicken.

- *"Arepa."*

    This is a common Venezuelan breakfast or afternoon Colombian snack that consists of a flat bread made with corn flour. They can be grilled, baked, or fried.

Let's take a look at Spanish food! In Spain, we will surely hear about the *"tortilla de patatas"*, *"la paella de mariscos"*, or the delicious *"croquetas"*. If so, you've probably wondered what its ingredients are, so let's learn the basics to cook the "*tortilla de patatas*"!

"Potato omelette." *"Tortilla de patatas."*
"Potato." *"Patata."* or *"papa"*
"Egg." *"Huevo."*
"Onion." *"Cebolla."*
"Salt." *"Sal."*
"Olive oil." *"Aceite de oliva."*

Now that you know the ingredients, let's review some basic instructions and kitchen elements to keep them in mind:

"Peel." *"Pelar."*
"Wash." *"Lavar."*
"Dry." *"Secar."*
"Cut." *"Cortar."*
"Cook." *"Cocinar."*
"Fire." *"Fuego."*
"Rest." *"Reposar."*

"Beat." *"Batir.*

"Frying pan." *"Sartén."*

"Bowl." *"Bol."*

Time to see how to prepare our omelette! In the following list, you will find the instructions:

1. *<u>Pelar</u> un kilo de <u>patatas</u>.*
2. *<u>Lavar</u>, <u>secar</u> y <u>cortar</u> las patatas.*
3. *Poner las patatas en un <u>bol</u> y poner <u>sal</u>.*
4. *Poner la <u>sartén</u> al <u>fuego</u> con <u>aceite de oliva</u>.*
5. *Poner las patatas para que se cocinen veinte minutos a fuego bajo.*
6. *<u>Batir</u> ocho <u>huevos</u> en el bol.*
7. *Pelar y cortar una <u>cebolla</u>.*
8. *En otra sartén, poner aceite de oliva y la cebolla.*
9. *Poner las patatas en el bol con los huevos y la cebolla. Dejar <u>reposar</u> quince minutos.*
10. *<u>Cocinar</u> la mezcla de los dos lados en la primera sartén.*

You may have understood most of it, but let's go over it one more time to make sure. The first thing you should do is peal "a kilo of potatoes" (*"un kilo de patatas"*). After that, you have to wash them well to remove traces of dirt and dry them. Place the potatoes in a large bowl and add salt to taste. Meanwhile, put the potatoes in a pan over the fire with olive oil and let it cook for twenty minutes. In the same bowl, beat eight eggs. Then peel and cut an onion cook it with olive oil in another pan. Add the potatoes and onion to the bowl with the eggs and let rest for fifteen minutes to finally cook the mixture on both sides in the first pan.

To end this section, let's look at some phrases that you might find useful:

- "I'm going to make seafood paella." *"Voy a preparar una paella de marisco."*
- "I like fried eggs." *"Me gustan los huevos fritos."*

CHAPTER 13:

HOLIDAY VOCABULARY

Christmas and New Year are some of the most popular Western celebrations, and Spanish speaking countries also enjoy these holidays.

While a white Christmas may not be as common in the warmer Spanish-speaking countries, they keep most of the regular traditions. Let's have a look at some common holidays greetings and wishes in Spanish:

- "Merry Christmas!" "*¡Feliz Navidad!*"
- "Happy holidays!" "*¡Felices fiestas!*"
- "Happy New Year!" "*¡Feliz Año Nuevo!*"
- "Merry Christmas and a happy New Year!" "*¡Feliz Navidad y próspero Año Nuevo!*"
- "Have a nice time this Christmas." "*Que pases lindo esta Navidad.*"
- "I wish you a Merry Christmas!" "*¡Te deseo una feliz Navidad!*"
- "All my best wishes for this Christmas!" "*¡Mis mejores deseos para esta Navidad!*"
- "I toast to… "*Brindo por…*"

Greetings are an important part of the holidays, but let's look at some more words to help expand our festive conversations:

"Santa Claus." "*Papá Noel.*" (He can also be called "*San Nicolás*".)

"Christmas Eve." "*La Nochebuena.*"

"Midnight." "*La medianoche.*"

"Christmas Day." "*El día de Navidad.*"

"The Christmas carol." "*Los villancicos.*"

"Chritmas tree." "*El árbol de Navidad.*"

"The decorations." "*Los adornos.*"

"The garland." "*La guirnalda.*"

"The mistletoe." "*El muérdago.*"

"The lights." "*Las luces.*"

"The presents." "*Los regalos.*"

"The cookies." "*Las galletas.*"

"The champagne." "*El champán.*"

"The cider." "*La cidra.*"

"The lamb." "*El cordero.*"

"The turkey." "*El pavo.*"

"Cheers!" "*¡Salud!*"

Now the following words have a special place in Spanish Christmas:
- "The nougat." "*El turrón.*" (it is a common food around Christmas time in most Spanish-speaking countries made of honey, eggwhite and sugar.)
- "*Los frutos secos.*" (this is the general term for nuts, almonds, etc.)
- "*El lechón*" (A pork-based dish, a young pig.)

Examples of its use:
- "On Christmas Eve, my family and I are going to eat a pork-based dish and sing carols." "*En Nochebuena, mi familia y yo vamos a comer lechón y cantar villancicos.*"
- "Santa Clause visited us at midnight." "*Papá Noel nos visitó a la medianoche.*"
- "My mom cooked the turkey and my younger brother made some cookies." "*Mi mamá cocinó el pavo y mi hermano menor hizo unas galletas.*"

Although Christmas is celebrated by people of many different faiths, it was originally a Christian holiday. This is also the case in Spanish-speaking countries, where the majority of the population follows the Christian religion. Whether or not you are a religious person, it will be valuable to know these common Christian phrases:

- "May God bless you!" "¡Que Dios te bendiga!"
- "At what time is mass held?" "¿A qué hora es la misa?"
- "Where is the mass held?" "¿Dónde es la misa?"
- "Baby Jesus." "El niño Jesús."
- "Virgin Mary." "La virgin María."
- "The Church." "La iglesia."
- "The nativity scene." "El pesebre."

Regardless of your beliefs or faith, Christmas is always a great time to get together with friends and family.

As for the New Year, let's look at some cultural curiosities. On New Years Eve, at twelve o'clock, most Spanish speakers eat twelve grapes. They all can feel the excitement! The bowls are prepared and they contain the grapes. Another tradition is to wear new clothes. So let's look at some vocabulary:

- "Twelve grapes." "Doce uvas."
- "New clothes." "Nueva ropa."

CHAPTER 14:

COMPOUND NOUNS

Most of the compound words in Spanish are formed with the union of a verb in the indicative in the third person of the singular followed by a plural noun or a singular noun.

In general, these nouns are the equivalent of verbs in English that are followed by a noun and ends in "-*er*", as in skyscraper, "*rascacielos*". This word starts with the verb "*rascar*" ("scratch") and its followed by "*cielos*" ("skies").

Although these words are usually hyphenated in English, they can also be written as a single word or two words. However, compound nouns in Spanish are always written as only one word.

For the most part, words formed in this way are masculine. Furthermore, the plural of these words remains identical to their singular form: a "skyscraper" is *"un rascacielos"* but if there are two or more the word still is *"los rascacielos"*.

The following list includes some of the most common compound words:

"The can-opener." *"El abrelatas."*
"The clothes closet." *"El guardarropas."* (It keeps clothing)
"The grasshopper." *"El saltamontes."* (It jumps hills)
"The lightning rod." *"El pararrayos."* (It stops lightning)
"The parachute." *"El paracaídas."* (It stops falls)
"The pen holder." *"El portaplumas."*

"The puzzle." "*El rompecabezas.*" (It breaks heads)

"The scarecrow." "*El espantapájaros.*" (It scares birds)

"The record-player." "*El tocadiscos.*"

"The tongue-twister." "*El trabalenguas.*"

"The umbrella." "*El paraguas.*" (It stops water)

As you have seen, in those cases in which the English translation omits the origin of the Spanish word, they will be accompanied by a literal translation.

The exception regarding the gender of the words formed in this way is those words used to refer to women or girls. So if we have a word like know-it-all, which means "*sabelotodo*", and we use it when talking about a woman, the article that precedes it will be "la". For example: "*la sabelotodo*" ("the know-it-all").

Notes

Notes

Notes

Notes

Notes

PART 2
VERBS AND SENTENCE STRUCTURE

CHAPTER 1:

SIMPLE PRESENT TENSE AND BASIC CONJUGATIONS FOR "AR" "ER" AND "IR" VERBS

It is time to learn the grammar of one of the first verb tenses that we will learn in this book, the simple present tense!

As in English, regular verbs are those that follow the same pattern as other verbs, with which they share endings. The verb stem ("-*ar*", "-*er*", or "-*ir*") will remain the same, while the ending will be replaced.

In both Spanish and English, we have regular infinitives and each of their endings ("-*ar*", "-*er*", and "-*ir*") will be cut off to be replaced by the present tense endings. We are going to do this by conjugating the verb so that we can know the different endings according to the person attached.

Let's start with the conjugation of the infinitives ending in "-*ar*":

Simple Present endings	Simple Present of *"hablar"*	Meaning
-o	*(Yo) hablo*	I speak
-as	*(tú) hablas*	You speak
-a	*(Él/ella/Usted) habla*	He/she/it speaks, you speak
-amos	*(Nosotros/nosotras) hablamos*	We speak

-an	*(Ellos/ellas/ustedes) hablan*	They/you speak

Example:

- "Carmen doesn't speak Spanish." "*Carmen no habla español.*"

Note that in general, you will not need to include the subject pronouns in Spanish, as the verb ending will make it clear who or what is doing the action.

Now let's see the conjugation of the infinitives ending in "*-er*":

Simple Present endings	Simple Present of *"comer"*	Meaning
-o	*(Yo) como*	I eat
-es	*(tú) comes*	You eat
-e	*(Él/ella/Usted) come*	He/she/it eats, you eat
-emos	*(Nosotros/nosotras) comemos*	We eat
-en	*(Ellos/ellas/ustedes) comen*	They/you eat

Example:

- "María and Paula eat too much." "*María y Paula comen demasiado.*"

Finally, we have the infinitives ending in "*-ir*":

Simple Present endings	Simple Present of *"escribir"*	Meaning
-o	*(Yo) escribo*	I write
-es	*(tú) escribes*	You write
-e	*(Él/ella/Usted) escribe*	He/she/it writes, you write
-imos	*(Nosotros/nosotras) escribimos*	We write
-en	*(Ellos/ellas/ustedes) escriben*	They/you write

Examples:

- "Martín opens the door." *"Martín aubre la puerta."*
- "We live in Canada." *"Vivimos en Canada."*

CHAPTER 2:

COMMON VERBS - PRESENT TENSE

In Spanish, the infinitive (verb form) is always made up of just one word (never two as in English) and ends in -ar, -er or -ir: for example, "*conversar*" (meaning to talk), "*beber*" (meaning to drink) and "*dormir*" (meaning to sleep).

But as in English, there are verbs in Spanish that don't follow the usual patterns. These **irregular verbs** include some of the most necessary verbs like, "*ser*" and "*estar*" (meaning to be). So, in this lesson, we will learn some regular and irregular verbs in Spanish starting with the verb "to be" that has two translations "*ser*" and "*estar*".

Verb to be	Verb "*ser*"	Verb "*estar*"
"I am"	Yo *soy*	Yo *estoy*
"You are"	Tú *eres*	Tú *estás*
"He/She/It is, You are"	Él/Ella/Usted *es*	Él/Ella/Usted *está*
"We are"	Nosotros *somos*	Nosotros *estamos*
"They/You are"	Ellos/Ellas/Ustedes *son*	Ellos/Ellas/Ustedes *están*

Now, we'll focus on five different uses of the verb "*ser*" that you can use to identify and describe people. Let's take a look.

Example 1: To identify someone (this is the most common way to introduce someone in Spanish):

- "Hi, Liam. She <u>is</u> my mom, Carmen. Mom, he <u>is</u> Liam." "*Hola, Liam. Ella <u>es</u> mi mamá, Carmen. Mamá, él <u>es</u> Liam.*"
- "He <u>is</u> my dog, Zeus." "*Él <u>es</u> mi perro, Zeus.*"

Example 2: To indicate the gender of a person

- "He <u>is</u> a man who is my neighbor." "*Él <u>es</u> un hombre que es mi vecino.*"

Example 3: To state someone's nationality

- "He <u>is</u> American." "*Él <u>es</u> estadounidense.*"
- "She <u>is</u> Argentinian." "*Ella <u>es</u> argentina.*"

Example 4: To describe physical or personality traits

- "My brother and his friend <u>are</u> tall." "*Mi hermano y su amigo <u>son</u> altos.*"
- "My sister <u>is</u> honest." "*Mi hermana <u>es</u> honesta.*"

Example 5: When/Where something takes place

- "Maria's flight <u>is</u> next Thursday." "*El vuelo de Maria <u>es</u> el próximo jueves.*"
- "The football game <u>is</u> in Madrid." "*El partido de fútbol <u>es</u> en Madrid.*"

Instead, the verb "*estar*" is used to describe the following:

Example 1: Temporary characteristics

- "Pablo <u>is</u> sad." "*Pablo <u>está</u> triste.*"
- "<u>I'm</u> happy." "*<u>Estoy</u> feliz.*"

Example 2: Marital status

- "She's single." "*Ella <u>está</u> soltera.*"
- "<u>I'm</u> married." "*<u>Estoy</u> casado.*"

Example 3: Where something is located

- "My uncle <u>is</u> in the hotel." "*Mi tío <u>está</u> en el hotel.*"
- "My friend is in Valencia." "*Mi amigo <u>está</u> en Valencia.*"

Example 4: in connection with modal adverbs

- "Going on a trip once a year is fine." "*Ir de viaje una vez al año está bien.*"

Example 5: preposition "*de*" + noun (express moods or situations)

- "Emilio is in a bad mood." "*Emilio está de mal humor.*"

Some of the most common (**regular**) verbs that you could use in your everyday life are:

Verb "to run"	Verb "*correr*"
I run	Yo *corro*
You run	Tú *corres*
He/She/It runs, You run	Él/Ella/Usted *corre*
We run	Nosotros *corremos*
They/You run	Ellos/Ellas/Ustedes *corren*

- "She runs very fast." "*Ella corre muy rapido.*"

Verb "to walk"	Verb "*caminar*"
I walk	Yo *camino*
You walk	Tú *caminas*
He/She/It walks, You walk	Él/Ella/Usted *camina*
We walk	Nosotros *caminamos*
They/You walk	Ellos/Ellas/Ustedes *caminan*

- "I walk every day." "*Yo camino todos los días.*"

Verb "to speak"	Verb "*hablar*"
I speak	Yo *hablo*
You speak	Tú *hablas*
He/She/It speaks, You speak	Él/Ella/Usted *habla*
We speak	Nosotros *hablamos*
They/You speak	Ellos/Ellas/Ustedes *hablan*

- "I speak Spanish." "*Yo hablo español.*"

Verb "to buy"	Verb "*comprar*"
I buy	Yo *compro*
You buy	Tú *compras*
He/She/It buys, You buy	Él/Ella/Usted *compra*
We buy	Nosotros *compramos*
They/You buy	Ellos/Ellas/Ustedes *compran*

- "My mom buys me cookies once a week." "*Mi mamá me compra galletas una vez a la semana.*"

Verb "to carry"	Verb "*llevar*"
I carry	Yo *llevo*
You carry	Tú *llevas*
He/She/It carries, You carry	Él/Ella/Usted *lleva*
We carry	Nosotros *llevamos*
They/You carry	Ellos/Ellas/Ustedes *llevan*

- "I carry the groceries, you take the box." "*Yo llevo los comestibles, tu toma la caja.*"

Verb "to eat"	Verb "*comer*"
I eat	Yo *como*
You eat	Tú *comes*
He/She/it eats, you eat	Él/Ella/Usted *come*
We eat	Nosotros *comemos*
They/You eat	Ellos/Elles/Ustedes *comen*

- "My brother <u>eats</u> pasta." "*Mi hermano <u>come</u> pasta.*"

Verb "to drink"	Verb "*beber*"
I drink	Yo *bebo*
You drink	Tú *bebes*
He/She/It drinks, You drink	Él/Ella/Usted *bebe*
We drink	Nosotros *bebemos*
They/You drink	Ellos/Ellas/Ustedes *beben*

- "My mom and my dad <u>drink</u> water." "*Mi mamá y mi papá <u>beben</u> agua.*"

Verb "to talk"	Verb "*conversar*"
I talk	Yo *converso*
You talk	Tú *conversas*
He/She/It talks, You talk	Él/Ella/Usted *conversa*
We talk	Nosotros *conversamos*
They/You talk	Ellos/Ellas/Ustedes *conversan*

- "José <u>talks</u> with Ana at work." "*José <u>conversa</u> con Ana en el trabajo.*"

Verb "to sleep"	Verb "*dormir*"
I sleep	Yo *duermo*
You sleep	Tú *duermes*
He/She/It sleeps, You sleep	Él/Ella/Usted *duerme*
We sleep	Nosotros *dormimos*
They/You sleep	Ellos/Ellas/Ustedes *duermen*

- "Every time I *sleep*, my neighbors make noise." "*Cada vez que <u>duermo</u>, mis vecinos hacen ruido.*"

It's time for us to meet **reflexive verbs** in Spanish. The way to distinguish reflexive verbs in Spanish is by looking at its end, because they all end in the pronoun *"se"* in their infinitive form. An example of it is the verb *"hablar"*, in which reflexive form means "to talk". Its reflexive form, *"hablarse"*, means "to talk to oneself." Nevertheless, the translations of Spanish reflexive verbs aren't always so straightforward.

1. "To wake up." "*Despertarse.*"

    "Everyday <u>I wake up</u> between half past seven and 8 o'clock." "*Todos los días <u>me despierto</u> entre las siete y media y las ocho en punto.*"

Conjugation of the verb "*despertarse*":

Verb "to wake up"	Verb "*despertarse*"
I wake up	(Yo) me *despierto*
You wake up	(Tú) te *despiertas*
He/She/It wakes up, You wake up	(Él/Ella/Usted) se *despierta*
We wake up	(Nosotros) nos *despertamos*
They/You wake up	(Ellos/Ellas/Ustedes) se *despiertan*

The Spanish noun *"baño"* means "bath," and the verb bañarse can mean "to take a bath" as well. However, since *"bañarse"* can also be the more general "to bathe," a person could also use this verb to express the event of them taking a shower. Here is an example of this reflexive verb:

2. "To take a bath." "*Bañarse.*"

    "One <u>bathes</u> every day." "*Uno <u>se baña</u> todos los días.*"

Conjugation of the verb "*bañarse*":

Verb "to take a bath"	Verb "bañarse"
I take a bath	(Yo) me *baño*
You take a bath	(Tú) te *bañas*
He/She/It takes a bath, You take	(Él/Ella/Usted) se *baña*
We take a bath	(Nosotros) nos *bañamos*
They/You take a bath	(Ellos/Ellas/Ustedes) se *bañan*

A situation worth noting is that if someone, at the beach, expresses their desire to "*bañarse*", they are telling you that they would like to take a swim (not wash themselves clean from sand). So remember, the Spanish reflexive verb "*bañarse*" can also mean "to go swimming".

- "Look at the waves! They are perfect <u>to go swimming</u>." "*¡Mira las olas! Están perfectas para <u>bañarse</u>.*"

When translating from Spanish to English, "*se*", "*me*" and so on are very rarely translated as "himself", "myself". Instead of "she dresses herself" or "I bathe myself", in English, we are more likely to say "she gets dressed" or "I have a bath".

But in Spanish the verb "*dormir*" and its reflexive form "*dormirse*" are not the same. "*Dormir*" refers to "to sleep" while "*dormirse*" as a pronominal verb referring to the action of "going to sleep/falling asleep".

Conjugation of the verb "*dormise*":

Verb "to fall asleep"	Verb "*dormirse*"
I go to sleep	(Yo) me *duermo*
You go to sleep	(Tú) te *duermes*
He/She/It goes to sleep, You go to sleep	(Él/Ella/Usted) se *duerme*
We go to sleep	(Nosotros) nos *dormimos*
They/You go to sleep	(Ellos/Ellas/Ustedes) se *duermen*

- "The baby <u>falls asleep</u> straight away." "*El bebé <u>se duerme</u> enseguida.*"

Let's see an example of the use of these verbs when describing situations like our daily routine:

- "Every Saturday I <u>wake up</u> late and have a cup of tea and cereal for breakfast. Then I go out for a walk and when I come back I <u>take a bath</u>. Then I go to sleep a few hours until it's time to make dinner."
  "Todos los sábados <u>me despierto</u> tarde y tomo una taza de té y cereales para el desayuno. Luego salgo a caminar y al regresar <u>me baño</u>. Entonces <u>me duermo</u> unas horas hasta que es la hora de hacer la cena."

CHAPTER 3:

SOME IRREGULAR VERBS - PRESENT TENSE

While we've already seen some other **irregular verbs**, we need to expand our vocabulary a bit more, so it's time to go over these other frequently used verbs:

Verb "to go"	Verb "*ir*"
I go	Yo *voy*
You go	Tú *vas*
He/She/It goes, You go	Él/Ella/Usted *va*
We go	Nosotros *vamos*
They/You go	Ellos/Ellas/Ustedes *van*

- "We go to the museum sometimes." "*Nosotros vamos al museo a veces.*"

Verb "to come"	Verb "*venir*"
I come	Yo *vengo*
You come	Tú *vienes*
He/She/It comes, You come	Él/Ella/Usted *viene*
We come	Nosotros *venimos*
They/You come	Ellos/Ellas/Ustedes *vienen*

- "My son comes to visit me once a month." "*Mi hijo viene a visitarme una vez al mes.*"

"Tener" means 'to have' and denotes ownership or possession.

Verb "to have"	Verb "*tener*"
I have	Yo *tengo*
You have	Tú *tienes*
He/She/It has, You have	Él/Ella/Usted *tiene*
We have	Nosotros *tenemos*
They/You have	Ellos/Ellas/Ustedes *tienen*

- "I have two sisters." "*Yo tengo dos hermanas.*"

Verb "to read"	Verb "*leer*"
I read	Yo *leo*
You read	Tú *lees*
He/She/It reads, You read	Él/Ella/Usted *lee*
We read	Nosotros *leemos*
They/You read	Ellos/Ellas/Ustedes *leen*

- "Every year, I read a lot of books." "*Todos los años leo muchos libros.*"

Verb "to want"	Verb "*querer*"
I want	Yo *quiero*
You want	Tú *quieres*
He/She/It wants, You want	Él/Ella/Usted *quiere*
We want	Nosotros *queremos*
They/You want	Ellos/Ellas/Ustedes *quieren*

- "We _want_ the blue one." "_Queremos el azul._"

Now, let's talk about verbs like "_gustar_". Even though it usually appears in the first weeks of learning Spanish, it is a tricky one. But don't worry because now we will solve this problem!

Verbs like "_gustar_" can be difficult for new learners of Spanish. This is because they need to be learned differently than the rest. These types of verbs are a little bit backwards so it is necessary to study them separately.

Verb "to like"	Verb "_gustar_"
I like	(A mí) me _gusta_
You like	(A ti) te _gusta_
He/She/It likes, You like	(A él) (A ella)(A usted) le _gusta_
We like	(A nosotros) nos _gusta_
They/You like	(A ellos)(A ellas)(A ustedes) les _gusta_

Notice a pattern? The indirect object pronouns are the ones that change according to who likes it, not the verbs. The verbs will change, but not according to the subject of the sentence as we are used to.

This verb is commonly used in the **third person singular** or **plural** to express "like":

- "I like the drawing." "_Me gusta el dibujo._" (singular form)
- "I like the drawings." "_Me gustan los dibujos._" (plural form).
- This verb is used with "_me_", "_te_", "_le_", "_nos_" and "_les_".

When learning Spanish, the confusion is that this Spanish verb defies the normal pattern that most verbs follow in both Spanish and English.

In place of following the form:

- person who likes + verb + object liked.

It follows this form:

- indirect object pronoun representing the person who likes + verb + object liked.

CHAPTER 4:

SIMPLE FUTURE

The simple future tense is used to talk about what will happen or shall happen. It is also used to talk about the possibility of what someone could or could not be doing in the present.

But there is good news! To form the simple future tense, you just need to add the correct ending to the infinitive of the verb. So all the verb conjugations (-*ar*, -*er*, and -*ir*) will share the same endings in the simple future tense. There are a few irregular verbs but for now, we will cover some regular ones.

Spanish Simple Future Endings:

Subject	Ending
Yo	-*é*
Tú	-*ás*
Él/Ellas/Usted	-*á*
Nosotros	-*emos*
Ellos/Ellas/Ustedes	-*án*

Check out these sentences with the simple future:

- "You will go to the party tonight." "*Irás a la fiesta esta noche.*"
- "She will see her mom tomorrow." "*Ella verá a su mamá mañana.*"

The simple future is most often used to talk about what a person will do, but it can also be used to talk about guesses, possibilities, and probabilities in the present, making predictions, or giving a command.

Examples of conjectures:

- "The children will eat lunch at noon." "*Los niños almorzarán al mediodía.*"
- "It must be seven o'clock in the morning." "*Serán las siete de la mañana.*"
- "They will buy a new house." "*Ellas comprarán una casa nueva.*"

Examples of predictions about the future:

- "I will marry a handsome man." "*Me casaré con un hombre guapo.*"
- "He will find a good job." "*Encontrará un buen trabajo.*"
- "She will write an amazing book." "*Ella escribirá un libro increíble.*"
- "We will all die one day." "*Todos moriremos un día.*"

Examples of solemn commands:

- "You will obey your grandparents." "*Obedecerás a tus abuelos.*"
- "You shall not steal." "*No robarás.*"
- "You will hear what I have to say." "*Escucharás lo que tengo para decir.*"
- "You will not eat the cake." "*No te comerás el pastel.*"

CHAPTER 5:

SIMPLE PAST

As we have said before, Spanish has 3 types of verbs ("*-ar*", "*-er*" and "*-ir*" verbs) with different conjugations. With the 'simple past' there is no difference between the second and third conjugation (the endings are the same).

- First Conjugation "*-ar*"

Verb "to walk"	Verb "*caminar*"
I walked	Yo *caminé*
You walked	Tú *caminaste*
He/She/It/You walked	Él/Ella/Usted *caminó*
We walked	Nosotros *caminamos*
They/You walked	Ellos/Ellas/Ustedes *caminaron*

Verb "to arrive"	Verb "*llegar*"
I arrived	Yo *llegué*
You arrived	Tú *llegaste*
He/She/It/You arrived	Él/Ella/Usted *llegó*
We arrived	Nosotros *llegamos*
They/You arrived	Ellos/Ellas/Ustedes *llegaron*

- Second Conjugation "-*er*"

Verb "to run"	Verb "*correr*"
I ran	Yo *corrí*
You ran	Tú *corriste*
He/she/It/You ran	Él/Ella/Usted *corrió*
We ran	Nosotros *corrimos*
They/You ran	Ellos/Ellas/Ustedes *corrieron*

Verb "to eat"	Verb "*comer*"
I ate	Yo *comí*
You ate	Tú *comiste*
He/She/It/You ate	Él/Ella/Usted *comió*
We ate	Nosotros *cominos*
They/You ate	Ellos/Ellas/Ustedes *comieron*

- Third Conjugation "-*ir*"

Verb "to sleep"	Verb "*dormir*"
I slept	Yo *dormí*
You slept	Tú *dormiste*
He/She/It/You slept	Él/Ella/Usted *durmió*
We slept	Nosotros *dormimos*
They/You slept	Ellos/Ellas/Ustedes *durmieron*

Verb "to write"	Verb "escribir"
I wrote	Yo *escribí*
You wrote	Tú *escribiste*
He/She/It/You wrote	Él/Ella/Usted *escribió*
We wrote	Nosotros *escribimos*
They/You wrote	Ellos/Ellas/Ustedes *escribieron*

The **simple past** is used for actions that didn't occur regularly at a particular time in the past. It is commonly used in stories and biographical writing, where there are sequences of events from the past.

Examples:

1. "Marina ran behind her dog until she caught it." "*Marina corrió detrás de su perro hasta que lo atrapó.*"
2. "I walked three blocks straight and found the library." "*Caminé tres cuadras seguidas y encontré la biblioteca.*"
3. "Today my younger sister slept in our parent's bedroom." "*Hoy mi hermana menor durmió en la habitación de nuestros padres.*"

Now, let's look at how to make questions with the simple past. When we ask a question, we usually change the position of the verb with the personal pronoun.

- While the affirmation would be "you slept" "*tú dormiste*", the question would be "did you sleep?" "*¿dormiste (tú)?*".

To obtain the negative form of it, simply add the word "no" before the verb.

- While the affirmation would be "you slept" "*tú dormiste*", the negation would be "you didn't sleep" "*tú no dormiste*".

CHAPTER 6:

IMPERFECT TENSE

In this section, we will see the imperfect tense. This is one of the verb tenses that is used to talk about the past (something that happened before today), especially when making descriptions, but also to say what was happening or used to happen. So, in other words, it is a way to describe how things used to be.

Examples:

- "We were living in Chile at the time." "*Vivíamos en Chile en ese momento.*"
- "It was cold." "*Hacía frío.*"

The Imperfect Tense verb endings for "-*ar*" are as follows: "aba", "abas", "aba", "ab*ámos*" and "aban". *All "ar" verbs have "aba" in the ending.*

Pronoun	"Hablar"	Meaning
Yo	*Hablaba*	I spoke I was speaking I used to speak
Tú	*Hablabas*	You spoke You were speaking You used to speak
Él / ella / usted	*Hablaba*	He / she / it / You spoke He / she / it was speaking You were speaking He / she / it / You used to speak
Nosotros / Nosotras	*Hablábamos*	We spoke We were speaking We used to speak
Ellos / ellas / ustedes	*Hablaban*	They / you spoke They / you were speaking They / you used to speak

Example:

- "We were studying Spanish." "*Nosotros estudiábamos español.*"

Something you may have noticed is that in the imperfect form of "-ar" verbs, the "nosotros" form of the conjugated verb has an accent.

Now, to form the imperfect form of those verbs ending in "-er" or "-ir" you must replace such endings with: "*ía*", "*-ías*", "*-ía*", "*-ían*", and "*-íamos*". All forms have a written accent over the "i".

Pronoun	"Comer"	"Vivir"	Meaning
Yo	*Comía*	*Vivía*	I ate / lived I was eating / living I used to eat / live
Tú	*Comías*	*Vivías*	You ate / lived You were eating / living You used to eat / live
Él / ella / usted	*Comía*	*Vivía*	He / she / it / you ate / lived He / she / it / you were eating / living He / she / it / you used to eat / live
Nosotros / Nosotras	*Comían*	*Vivían*	We ate / lived We were eating / living We used to eat / live
Ellos / ellas / ustedes	*Comían*	*Vivían*	They / you ate / lived They / you were eating / living They / you used to eat / live

Example:

- "Mario used to live in a house in Buenos Aires." *"Mario vivía en una casa en Buenos Aires."*

CHAPTER 7:

"SER" AND "ESTAR"

There are two verbs in Spanish that mean "to be": "*ser*" and "*estar*". But as with the other verbs, we cannot simply say "*ser*" or "*estar*" with everyone. We must conjugate them.

Pronoun	"Ser"	Meaning
Yo	Soy	I am
Tú	Eres	You are
Él / ella / Usted	Es	He/she/it is, you are
Nosotros / Nosotras	Somos	We are
Ellos / ellas / ustedes	Son	They/you are

Usually this verb appears in the following situations:

- When it is a permanent condition, that is, it does not change. Example: "That house is big." "*Esa casa es grande.*"
- It is also used when talking about people's occupations. Example: "She is a vet." "*Ella es veterinaria.*"
- Another use of the verb "*ser*" is when mentioning the place of origin of someone or something. Example: "I'm from Spain." "*Yo soy de españa.*"
- When we identify something or someone (characteristics). Example: "Manuel is tall." "*Manuel es alto.*"

- Finally, we can use this verb to say our nationality. Example: "We are Canadians." "*Nosotros somos canadienses.*"

Now that we have reviewed the verb "*ser*", we are ready to take a look at the second form of the verb "to be".

Pronoun	*Estar*	Meaning
Yo	Estoy	I am
Tú	Estás	You are
Él / ella / usted	Está	He/she/it is, you are
Nosotros / Nosotras	Estamos	We are
Ellos / ellas / ustedes	Estan	They/you are

To be able to differentiate when you should use each of these verbs, you must remember the following conditions under which "estar" is used.

- When the conditions are temporary as is the case with feelings. Example: "I am sad." "*Estoy triste.*"
- The other use is when we talk about locations (even if these are permanent as can be a city). Example: "I'm at home." "*Estoy en casa.*"

Even if both "*ser*" and "*estar*" can be used with some adjectives, the meaning will change depending on which is used.

CHAPTER 8:

"POR" AND "PARA"

It's time to pay attention to some of the most used prepositions in Spanish!

When using the words "*por*" and "*para*", keep in mind that the first is used to explain the cause or motive of something, while the second usually refers to the purpose of an action.

Now, it may be useful to remember that both words have a few meanings. Let's start with "*por*":

- When we want to express a benefit or the reason for something, "*por*" can mean "for" (because of). Example: "She does it for him." "*Ella lo hace por él.*"
- In the same way, "*por*" can mean "for" when talking about an exchange (in exchange for). Example: "How much will you give me for this videogame?" "*¿Cuánto me darás por este videojuego?*"
- On the other hand, when passive constructions are made, "*por*" can mean "by". Example: "Found by his wife." "*Encontrado por su esposa.*"
- When talking about transports, "*por*" can also mean "by". Example: "Came by train." "*Vino por tren.*"
- "*Por*" can be used when indicating where something or someone is located in a vague way. Example: "I looked for Rosa everywhere." "*Busqué a Rosa por todas partes.*"
- It can also mean "around". Example: "To walk around the park." "*Caminar por el parque.*"

- Another situation in which you might find yourself with the use of "*por*" is when we are talking about time. Example: "In the morning." "*Por la mañana.*"
- "*Por*" can be used to talk about rates. Example: "Ten per cent." "*Diez por ciento.*"
- As we mentioned before, you may find it used in phrases that express the reason for something. Example: "For that reason." "*Por esa razón.*"
- Finally, "*por*" can appear in conversations about things that are already done. Example: "I heard it on the radio." "*Lo oí por la radio.*"

As for the word "*para*", its most common uses are:

1. When talking about a person, destination or purpose, it can mean "for". Example: "She leaves for London at three in the afternoon. "*Ella sale para Londres a las tres de la tarde.*"
2. With time, "*para*" can mean "for". Example: "*The homework is for tomorrow.*" "*La tarea es para mañana.*"
3. Another common use for the word "*para*" is accompanied by an infinitive that means "(in order) to". Example: "I did it to win the prize." "*Lo hice para ganar el premio.*"

One last difference between Spanish and English that you may have noticed is that in the former you cannot end sentences with a preposition, as in the latter. It is however, less formal to end a sentence with a preposition in English.

CHAPTER 9:

BASIC ADVERBS

An adverb is a word that modifies verbs, adjectives or other adverbs that gives more information about when, how, where, or in what circumstances something happens, or to what degree something is true, for example, "quickly", "happily" and "normally". Adverbs can modify verbs, adjectives and other adverbs but never nouns.

Different **groups of adverbs** are there to answer different questions. For example:

- Adverbs that describe "where?" For example:
  "Here." "*Aquí.*"
  "There." "*Allí.*"
  "Close." or "Near." "*Cerca.*"

- Adverbs that describe "when?" For example:
  "Today." "*Hoy.*"
  "Yesterday." "*Ayer.*"
  "Tomorrow." "*Mañana.*"

- Adverbs of frequency describe "how often?" For example:
  "Always." "*Siempre.*"
  "Never." "*Nunca.*"
  "Sometimes." "*A veces.*"

Degree adverbs are the most common types of modifiers of adjectives and other adverbs. The following adverbs express degrees of qualities, states, properties, conditions, and relations:

"A (little) bit." "*Un poco.*"
"A lot." "*Mucho.*"
"Very." "*Muy.*"
"Quite." "*Bastante.*"
"Somewhat." "*Algo.*"
"Too." "*Demasiado.*"

Adverbs in Spanish always come before or after the word they modify.

For example:

- "Camila eats a lot." "*Camila come mucho.*" (here "*mucho*" modifies the verb "*comer*")
- "Carlos is very handsome." "*Carlos es muy guapo.*" (here "*muy*" modifies the adjective "*guapo*")
- "You are speaking too fast." "*Estás hablando demasiado rápido.*" (here "*demasiado*" modifies the adjective "*rápido*")

When modifying an adjective you always have to place the adverb in front of the adjective. Let's have a look at some examples:

- "Very." "*Muy.*"
  "Your daughter is very tall." "*Tu hija es muy alta.*"

- "Too." "*Demasiado.*"
  "This car is too expensive." "*Este coche es demasiado caro.*"

- "Somewhat." "*Algo.*"
  "You are somewhat pale." "*Estás algo pálido.*"

Since adverbs can modify adverbs too, you should be clear that the general rule also applies here. Again, the adverb that makes the modification must always be placed before the modified one:

- "Pablo swims quite frequently." "*Pablo nada con bastante frecuencia.*"

An adverb can also modify a whole sentence. In this case, it can be placed at the beginning or at the end of that sentence:

- "We will go to the hospital tomorrow." "*Iremos al hospital mañana.*"
- "Tomorrow we will go to the hospital." "*Mañana iremos al hospital.*"

English adverbs are often formed by adding -ly to an adjective, for example: "sad" turns into "sadly", and are used to explain how something happened. But in Spanish, to form a similar adverb you need to add *-mente* to **the feminine singular** form of the adjective.

Examples:

Masculine Adjective	Feminine Adjective	Adverb	Meaning
"Lento"	"Lenta"	"Lentamente"	Slowly
"Rápido"	"Rápida"	"Rápidamente"	Quickly
"Normal"	"Normal"	"Normalmente"	Normally

You don't have to worry about adding or removing accents on the adjective when you add *-mente*; they stay as they are:

"Easy." "*Fácil.*" turns into "Easily." "*Fácilmente.*"

These are some examples of its use:

- "My grandfather speaks very slowly." "*Mi abuelo habla muy lentamente.*"
- "Do it quickly!" "*¡Hazlo rápidamente!*"
- "I normally arrive at nine o'clock." "*Normalmente llego a las nueve.*"

As you have probably noticed, adverbs don't change their endings in Spanish to agree with anything (neither quantity nor gender).

Another rule worth knowing, when there are two or more adverbs joined by a conjunction such as "*y*" (meaning "and") or "*entonces*" (meaning "so"), you need to leave out the *-mente* ending on all but the last adverb.

- "They did it slowly but efficiently." *"Lo hicieron lenta pero eficazmente."* (here, the last adverb is *"eficazmente"* which comes from the adjective *"eficaz"*)

In Spanish, adverbs ending in *-mente* aren't as common as adverbs ending in -ly in English. Therefore, there are other ways to express adverbs in Spanish, for example, "*con*" used with a noun or "*de manera*" used with an adjective.

Examples:

- "Drive carefully." *"Conduce con cuidado."*
- "All these changes happen naturally." *"Todos estos cambios ocurren de manera natural."*

In the case of **irregular adverbs**, things are quite different. For example, the adverb that comes from "good", "*bueno*", is "*bien*" which means "well". The adverb that comes from "bad", "*malo*" is "*mal*", which means "badly".

Examples:

- "He speaks Spanish well." *"Habla bien el español."*
- "It's a good movie." *"Es una buena película."*
- "It's very badly written." *"Está muy mal escrito."*
- "This is a bad show." *"Este es un show malo."*

Additionally, there are some other adverbs in Spanish which stay exactly the same like "*alto*" (adjective: "high", "loud"; adverb: "high", "loudly") and "*bajo*" (adjective: "low", "quiet"; adverb: "low", "quietly").

Examples:

- "The plane flew high over the mountains." *"El avión volaba alto sobre las montañas."*
- "Martin talks very loudly." *"Martín habla muy alto."*
- "The car was driving very fast." *"El coche iba muy rápido."*
- "Speak quietly!" *"¡Habla bajo!"*

Some other irregular verbs are *"fuerte"* (which is synonymous with the words "strong", "loud" and "hard") and "straight", *"derecho"*:

- "Don't hit the door so hard." *"No golpees la puerta tan fuerte."*
- "He talks very loudly." *"Habla muy fuerte."*
- "He came straight towards me." *"Vino derecho hacia mí."*

But often you will be able to use an adverb or an adverbial expression equally in Spanish:

- "They were waiting impatiently." could be *"Esperaban impacientemente."* or *"Esperaban con impaciencia."*

CHAPTER 10:

HOW TO BUILD SENTENCES AND SOME COMMON CONNECTORS

Since the structure of sentences in Spanish is not the same as in English, here are some rules for constructing basic sentences. All Spanish sentences need a subject and a verb.

First we will talk about the subject:

So, if our subject is "Carlos", and our verb is "*leer*", which means "to read", we can then make the simple sentence:

- "Carlos reads." "*Carlos lee.*"

And, to make things even easier, it's often possible to omit the subject once we know who we are talking about. So if we said "*Carlos lee,*" our next sentence could be,

- "He reads." "*Lee*"

You can add an adverb after the verb to further describe the action:

- "He reads a lot." "*Lee mucho.*"

The second rule is that if you want to make a Spanish sentence negative, you just need to add "*no*" before the verb. Let's look at the negative of "*Carlos lee*":

- "Carlos doesn't read." "*Carlos no lee.*"

You can add to the sentence from your building block and use the verb "preferir" which means "to prefer":

- "Carlos doesn't read because he prefers to draw." *"Carlos no lee porque prefiere dibujar."*

Another curiosity of Spanish is that, unlike English, it is possible to use double negatives:

- *"No me gusta nada"* is a sentence that translates literally to, "I don't like nothing," but is completely correct grammatically in Spanish.

Now, if your conversation isn't going to be one-sided, you'll also likely want to ask questions. So here is the third and last rule that we are going to see in this lesson: there are three ways to make questions in Spanish.

1. Switch verb and subject

    - "Carlos draws", *"Carlos dibuja"*, becomes "Does Carlos draw?" *"¿Dibuja Carlos?"*

    Also, don't forget that the Spanish question needs both question marks. One upside down at the beginning and the usual one at the end.

2. Add question marks and rising intonation

    This way is even easier. The only thing you have to do (while writing) to make a question is to put question marks around a statement.

    - *"Carlos dibuja."* becomes *"¿Carlos dibuja?"*

    But if you are talking you will also have to pay attention to the intonation and go up at the end of the sentence so the other person will know that it is a question.

3. Add question tags

    In this case you will add a questions word after the sentence like in English. Easy, right?

- *"Carlos dibuja."* becomes *"Carlos dibuja, ¿no?"* (This is like saying "Carlos draws, doesn't he?" or *"Carlos dibuja, ¿verdad?"*

Another important part of sentences is the comma. Most of the time the comma in Spanish is used much like the comma in English. There are differences, however, especially for lists or in the case of comments that are inserted within sentences.

At the same time, you can use a comma in the case of explanatory phrases and the rule for it is much the same as it is in English. So a phrase that is used to describe something, will be set off by commas. But when it's used to define what is being referred to, will be not. For example:

- "The car that is in the garage is red." *"El carro que está en el garaje es roja."* (Commas aren't needed because the explanatory phrase *"que está en el garaje"* is telling us which car is being discussed.)

However, the same sentence punctuated differently would not intend to tell the reader which truck is being discussed but to describe where it is:

- "The car, which is in the garage, is red." *"El carro, que está en el garaje, es roja."*

When a phrase or word is immediately followed by another phrase or word that is referring to the same overlapping concept, (called an apposition), it is similarly punctuated much as in English. Let's see the difference between these examples:

- "I love my cat, Bubbles." *"Amo a mi gato, Bubbles."* (I have one cat, and his name is Bubbles.)
- "I love my cat Bubbles." *"Amo a mi gato Bubbles."* (I have more than one cat, and I love Bubbles.)

When quotation marks are used, the comma goes outside the quotation marks, unlike American English:

- *"Los familiares no comprendieron la ley", aclaró el abogado.* ("The family members did not understand the law," the lawyer clarified.)
- *"Muchos no saben distinguir entre ambas cosas", dijo Dieguez.* (Many do not know how to distinguish between both things, Dieguez said.)

Commas can also be used to highlight exclamations that are inserted within a sentence. The English equivalent would be the long dashes.

- "The new Pope — I can't believe it! — is a native of Argentina." "*El nuevo presidente, ¡no lo creo!, es oriundo de Argentina.*"

Another rule you will need to remember when writing is that a comma should always precede conjunctions that mean "except." The most common words for this are "*excepto*", "*salvo*" and "*menos*":

- "I love all living beings except bugs." "*Amo a todos los seres vivos, excepto a los bichos.*"
- "I have excellent grades in all subjects except math." "*Tengo excelentes calificaciones en todas las materias, excepto en matemáticas.*"

Commas are also intended to separate adverbs or adverbial phrases (that affect the meaning of the entire sentence) from the rest of the sentence. These words and phrases usually appear at the beginning of a sentence, but they can also be found inserted within the sentence:

- "However, I think you're very talented." "*Sin embargo, pienso que eres muy talentoso.*"
- "Of course, I understand it." "*Por supuesto, lo comprendo.*"
- "Child poverty, unfortunately, is a reality." "*Pobreza infantil, desgraciadamente, es una realidad.*"

Joining two sentences in Spanish is usually done with "*y*" and in English "and" is used. In these cases, you should use a comma before the conjunction.

- "Unlike dogs, cats don't need to go for a walk every day, and that makes their sedentary attitude worse." "*A diferencia de los perros, los gatos no necesitan salir a pasear todos los días, y eso empeora su actitud sedentaria.*"
- "The Moon takes the same time to rotate on its axis as it does to orbit the Earth, a little over twenty-seven days, and that is why we always see the same hemisphere." "*La Luna tarda el mismo tiempo en girar sobre su eje que en orbitar la Tierra, un poco más de veintisiete días, y por eso siempre vemos el mismo hemisferio.*"

However, if the compound sentence is very short, the comma can be omitted:

- "I love apples and I love oranges." "*Me encantan* las *manzanas y me encantan las naranjas.*"

There are some differences with commas and numbers. In Spain, South America, and parts of Central America, the comma and period are used in numbers in the reverse way that they are in American English. Thus "*134,658,769.01*" in English becomes "134.658.769,01" in most Spanish speaking areas. However, in Mexico, Puerto Rico and parts of Central America, the American English convention is followed.

A comma shouldn't be used to separate the subject of a sentence from the main verb unless it is necessary to separate apposition words or intermediate phrases, a rule shared with English:

Examples:

- "The last year was very difficult." "*El último año fue muy difícil.*" (This is correct.)
- "The last year, was very difficult." "*El último año, fue muy difícil.*" (This is incorrect.)

Now that you know how to make a sentence and the rules for how to use commas, let's talk about **Spanish Linking Words** or "*los conectores*", which are crucial words or groups of words that join ideas by clearly expressing how they relate to each other. We need to incorporate them because the proper use of connectors will give greater coherence to our discourse and will make it more intelligible for those who listen or read. Let's check the main categories of connectors!

Temporary and Sequence:

Temporary linking words are used to place actions or events in time, either concerning other actions or facts or to the moment in which the speaker talks.

Sequential linking words can be used to present an ordered series of ideas or arguments, by establishing a sequence or by ranking the ideas according to their importance:

- "At the beginning..." "*Al principio...*"
- "Before..." "*Antes (de)...*"
- "Afterwards..." or "Then..." are "*Después (de)...*" and "*Luego...*"
- "At the same time..." "*Al mismo tiempo...*"
- "Finally..." "*Finalmente...*"
- "Firstly..." "*Primero...*"
- "Lastly..." "*Por último...*"
- "In conclusion..." "*En conclusión...*"
- "To summarise..." "*Para resumir...*"
- "Then..." "*Entonces...*"
- "Later..." "*Luego...*"

Examples:

- "<u>First</u>, I shower so <u>later</u> I can have breakfast." "*<u>Primero</u> me ducho para <u>luego</u> poder desayunar.*"
- "<u>Before</u> going to sleep I always brush my teeth." "*<u>Antes de</u> ir a dormir siempre me cepillo los dientes.*"

Cause: express the cause or reason for something.

- "Because..." "*Porque...*"
- "Due to..." "*Debido a (que)...*"
- "As..." "*Como...*"
- "Because of..." "*A causa de (que)...*"

Examples:

- "Pilar works a lot <u>because</u> she likes her work." "*Pilar trabaja mucho <u>porque</u> le gusta su trabajo.*"
- "I'm not as advanced in Spanish <u>as</u> you." "*No soy tan avanzado en español <u>como</u> tú.*"
- "<u>Because</u> I am from Argentina, there is no snow on New Year." "*<u>Porque</u> soy de Argentina, no hay nieve en Año Nuevo.*"

Opposition: introduce opposing, contradictory, or incompatible ideas. They are used to formulate an opposition, a restriction, or an objection.

- "But…" "*Pero*"
- "However…" "*Sin embargo…*"
- "Although…" "*Aunque…*"
- "Nevertheless…" "*No obstante…*"
- "Despite…" "*A pesar de (que)…*"

Examples:

- "Micaela is great in math <u>but</u> not so great at English." "*Micaela es genial en matemáticas <u>pero</u> no tanto en inglés.*"
- "<u>Although</u> we don't have much, we are very happy." "*<u>Aunque</u> no tenemos mucho, somos muy felices.*"
- "<u>Despite</u> liking dogs better, cats do seem cute to me." "*<u>A pesar de que</u> me gustan más los perros, los gatos me parecen lindos.*"

Addition:

- "And…" "*Y…*"
- "Also…" "*Además…*"
- "Too…" "*También…*"
- "Even…" "*Incluso…*"
- "As well as…" "*Además de…*"

Examples:

1. "I have a cat <u>and</u> two dogs." "*Tengo un gato <u>y</u> dos perros.*"
2. "I like pizza <u>too</u>!" "*¡A mí <u>también</u> me gusta la pizza!*"
3. "Today was a bad day; I fell asleep and was late for work. <u>Also</u>, I stained my favorite tie." "*Hoy fue un mal día, me quedé dormido y llegué tarde al trabajo. <u>Además</u>, manché mi corbata favorita.*"

CHAPTER 11:

GREETINGS AND HOW TO INTRODUCE YOURSELF

There are a variety of phrases that you may want to keep handy while starting with Spanish. Regardless of whether you are meeting/greeting someone, ordering, or shopping at a local market, incorporating some of these expressions into your early vocabulary repertoire will help take your Spanish to the next level and above all, get you talking faster!

The first thing that you may want to say to someone is "hello", "*hola*". But also "nice to meet you", "*mucho gusto*", or "*encantado*". In the case of the last one, it will end with an "*o*" or an "*a*" depending on who says it.

Now, before we go any further, we will continue with a simple Spanish question:

- "How are you?" "*¿Qué tal?*" o "*¿Cómo estás?*"
  These are one of the easiest ways to ask someone "How are you feeling?" or "How is it going?" You can also combine them: "*Hola, ¿qué tal?*"

Remember that Spanish has formal and informal forms of "you":

- "*Tú*" is used when talking to people you know, like your friends, or people the same age as you or younger. "*Usted*" is the way to refer to someone when you don't know them, to someone who is older, or to whom you wish to show respect and formality. That is, if you want to refer to someone as "*usted*", the question "how are you?" would be done in the following way: "*¿cómo está?*"

The possible answers for that question may be:

"Great!" "¡Genial!"
"Good!" "¡Bien!"
"So so." "Más o menos."
"Bad." "Mal."
"Terrible!" "¡Terrible!"

This can be accompanied by the question "what about you?" "¿y tú?". Now, let's look at an example of these words in everyday use:

1. **Formal**

   Q: "Hi! How are you?" "¡Hola! ¿Cómo está usted?"

   A: "Good, thanks. And you?" "Bien, gracias. ¿Y usted?"

2. **Informal**

   Q: "How are you feeling" "¿Cómo estás?"

   A: "So so, my sister and I fought today." "Más o menos, mi hermana y yo peleamos hoy."

No matter what your native language is, simple courtesies are always very helpful. These Spanish phrases will ensure you have a pleasant conversation:

"Thank you!" "¡Gracias!"
"Thank you very much!" "¡Muchas gracias!"
"Welcome!" "¡De nada!"
"Please" "Por favor"
"Excuse me!" "¡Disculpe!" (to apologize in advance for being in the way or bothersome)
"Sorry!" "¡Lo siento!" (to apologize for doing something wrong)

Greetings are a basic form of courtesy in society. They are a common way to show someone new that you are friendly and respectful. That's why it's so important to learn how to greet someone in each type of social situation, whether they are very formal or very informal. Listen to these greetings and try to repeat them outloud:

"Good morning!" "¡Buenos días!"
"Good afternoon!" "¡Buenas tardes!"
"Good night!" "¡Buenas noches!"

Let's imagine you are meeting a group of Spanish speakers, you might wave and say a quick "hello!", "¡hola!", right? But that will not cover the whole group. To be polite, you'll have to greet and introduce yourself to everyone individually. To do so, you can say:

- "My name is…" "Me llamo..." or "Mi nombre es..."
- "I am…" "Soy…"
  "Soy" is sometimes used as an alternative to "me llamo". It's especially suited to casual encounters.

Now when it comes to meeting someone, we all want to know a little more about the person in question, so these are some of the questions that could most likely come up in the conversation:

- "Where are you from?" "¿De dónde eres?"
  This can easily be answered by simply saying your nationality ("I'm American." "Soy americana.", "I'm Russian.", "Soy ruso.", etc.), or where you come from (I'm from the U.S." "Soy de Estados Unidos.", "I'm from Russia." "Soy de Rusia.", etc.).

- "Where do you live?" "¿Dónde vives?"
  The simplest answer is composed with "I live…" + "in" + place: "I live in Madrid." "Vivo en Madrid."

- "How old are you?" "¿Qué edad tienes?"
  The answer is "I am ..." + age number, like this: "I'm twenty-two years old." "Tengo veintidós años."

If you want to be friendly to a stranger, sometimes it's better to include something interesting about yourself. You can mention your hobbies, your bucket list, you favourite movie, or other things that you enjoy doing.

Talking about ones hobbies *"pasatiempos"* are a great way to get to know someone. Fishing, working out, traveling, gardening, camping, cooking, reading, learning languages, watching movies, and playing an instrument are all on the following list:

"Painting." *"Pintar."*

"Fishing." *"Pescar."*

"Cooking." *"Cocinar."*

"Playing video games." *"Jugar videojuegos."*

"Camping." *"Acampar."*

"Learning a new language." *"Aprender un nuevo idioma."*

"Doing yoga." *"Hacer yoga."*

"Traveling." *"Viajar."*

"Reading." *"Leer."*

"Playing an instrument." *"Tocar un instrumento."*

"Arts and crafts." *"Artes y manualidades."*

"Gardening." *"Jardinería."*

"Working out." *"Hacer ejercicio."*

This is how complete presentations examples would look:

A: "Hi, my name is Carlos Garcia. I am twenty-four years old and I am from Argentina." *"Hola, mi nombre es Carlos Garcia. Tengo veinticuatro años y soy de Argentina."*

B: "Nice to meet you! My name is Rafael. I am forty years old." *"¡Mucho gusto! Mi nombre es Oswald. Tengo cuarenta años."*

A: "Where are you from, Oswald?" *"¿De dónde eres, Rafael?"*

B: "I was born in the United States, but nowadays I reside in Valencia. Do you have any hobbie?" *"Nací en Estados Unidos, pero actualmente vivo en Valencia. ¿Tienes algún pasatiempo?"*

A: "I'm into camping and working out! What about you?" *"¡Me gusta acampar y hacer yoga! ¿Qué hay de ti?"*

B: "Fishing is what I love." *"¡Pescar es lo que me gusta!"*

Saying goodbye can be hard, especially if you don't know how to do it properly. So here are some popular Spanish phrases that will help you to end any conversation:

"Goodbye!" "*¡Adiós!*"

"See you later!" "*¡Hasta luego!*" (most likely today)

"See you tomorrow!" "*¡Hasta mañana!*"

"See you!" "*Nos vemos.*" (informal)

"Take care!" "*¡Cuídate!*"

"Have a good trip!" "*¡Buen viaje!*"

Something interesting is that intonation is what matters the most when we are asking questions in Spanish. Once you know that, you can transform a statement into a Yes/No. As we saw before, the structure for these kinds of Spanish questions is the following:

- ¿ + (subject) + conjugated verb + (additional information) + ?

Example:

1. **Statement**

    "Marco likes to eat pizza." "*A Marco le gusta comer pizza.*"

    Question

    Does Marco like to eat pizza? "*¿A Marco le gusta comer pizza?*"

2. **Statement**

    "You want to go shopping." "*Quieres ir de compras.*"

    Question

    "Do you want to go shopping?" "*¿Quieres ir de compras?*"

If you want to make a negative question, you just need to add a "no" before the conjugated verb.

3. **Statement**

    "You don't like to study." "*No te gusta estudiar.*"

    Question

    "Don't you like to study?" "*¿No te gusta estudiar?*"

Here are the Spanish question words for 'what', 'which', 'when', 'where', 'who', 'why' and 'how':

1. "What" "Qué"
   "What time is it?" "¿Qué hora es?"

2. "Which" "Cuál"
   "Which glass was yours?" "¿Qué vaso era tuyo?"

3. "When" "Cuándo"
   "When do you finish college?" "¿Cuándo terminas la universidad?"

4. "Where" "Dónde"
   "Where are you from?" "¿De dónde eres?"

5. "Who" "Quién"
   "Who is it?" "¿Quién es?"

6. "Why "Por qué"
   "Why are you saying that?" "¿Por qué dices eso?"

7. "How "Cómo"
   "What's your name?" "¿Cómo te llamas?"

CHAPTER 12:

TELLING TIME

Believe it or not, there are several useful formulas you may want to know to help yourself tell time with the verb *"ser"* in Spanish.

"One o'clock" *"la una"*, is the only hour used with the **third person singular** form of *"ser"*.

Examples:

- *"es"* + *"la"* + *"una"* (+ number of minutes)
  "It's one thirty." *"Es la una treinta."*

- *"es"* + *"la"* + *"una"* (+ *"y"* + number of minutes)
  "It's one twenty." *"Es la una y veinte."*

- *"es"* + *"la"* + *"una"* (+ *"con"* + number of minutes)
  "It's one forty." *"Es la una con cuarenta."*

This formula can be used to say It's (number of minutes) until (a certain hour):

- *"es"* + *"la"* + *"una"* + *"menos"* (+ number of minutes)
  "It's ten 'til one." *"Es la una menos diez."*

Unlike English, whose literal meaning is "ten minutes to one," in Spanish the literal meaning would be "one o'clock minus ten minutes".

From two to twelve o'clock the following formulas are used with the **third person plural** form of *"ser"*.

Examples:

- *"son"* + *"las"* + number from two to twelve (+ number of minutes)
  "It's three ten." *"Son las tres diez."*

- *"son"* + *"las"* + number from two to twelve (+ *"y"* + number of minutes)
  "It's nine twenty-nine." *"Son las nueve y veintinueve."*

- *"son"* + *"las"* + number from two to twelve (+ *"con"* + number of minutes)
  "It's ten ten." *"Son las diez con diez."*

The next formula (which is really similar) can be used to say It's (number of minutes) until (a certain hour):

- *"Son"* + *"las"* + number from two to twelve + *"menos"* (+ number of minutes)
  "It's five to nine." *"Son las nueve menos cinco."*

To indicate that it's half past the hour in Spanish, use the phrase *"y media"* like this:

- "It's seven thirty." *"Son las siete y media."*

If you want to say that it's a quarter past the hour, use the phrase *"y cuarto"*:

- "It's one fifteen." or "It's a quarter after one." *"Es la una y cuarto."*

To indicate that it's a quarter to the hour, use the word *"menos"* as in the last formula:

- "It's a quarter to five." *"Son las cinco menos cuarto."*

Here are some expressions that you can use regularly when describing time:

"In the (early) morning." *"De la madrugada."*
"In the morning." *"De la mañana."*
"In the afternoon." *"De la tarde."*
"In the evening." *"De la noche."*
"Around." *"Más o menos."*
"Noon." *"Mediodía."*
"Midnight." *"Medianoche."*

Examples of its use:

- "It's four in the morning. Go to sleep!" *"Son las dos de la madrugada. ¡Vete a dormir!"*
- "It's one in the afternoon." *"Es la una de la tarde."*
- "It's around nine o'clock." *"Son las nueve más o menos."*

CHAPTER 13:

THE WEATHER

The weather is something everyone knows, and everyone has an opinion, which makes it a great conversation piece when you first learn Spanish.

Describing the weather in Spanish can be divided up three main ways:

1. Situations when the weather "does":
   For this kind of phrase you will use the verb *"hacer"*, which usually means "to do" or "to make", in order to express what the weather "does".

   - "It's hot." *"Hace calor."*
   - "It's cold." *"Hace frío."*
   - "It's cool." *"Hace fresco."*

   And sometimes, the weather is easliy described like this:

   - "The weather is good." *"Hace buen tiempo."*
   - "The weather is bad." *"Hace mal tiempo."*

2. Times when the weather "is":
   In the case of the following weather conditions, you need to use the verb *"estar"* because as you may remember, it is used to talk about a non-permanent state, like the weather!

   - "It's cloudy." *"Está nublado."*
   - "It's sunny." *"Está soleado."*

- "It's clear." "*Está despejado.*"
- "It's windy." "*Está ventoso.*"
- "It's stormy." "*Está tormentoso.*"
- "It's raining." "*Está lloviendo.*"
- "It's snowing." "*Está nevando.*"

3. Times when "there is" some kind of weather:

   Lastly, there are times when the verb form "*hay*" is used to indicate that there is some kind of unusual weather occurring:

   - "It's windy (literally "there is wind")." "*Hay viento.*"
   - "It's foggy (literally "there is fog")." "*Hay niebla.*"

Examples of everyday use:

1. "The weather is nice today. It's sunny and the sky is clear." "*El clima es agradable hoy. Hace sol y el cielo está despejado.*"
2. "I can't see the route! It's too foggy." "*¡No veo la ruta! Hay demasiada niebla.*"
3. "I love days like today, rainy and cool." "*A mi, me gustan los días como hoy, lluviosos y frescos.*"
4. "It's so windy that my hat flew away." "*Hace tanto viento que mi sombrero se fue volando.*"

The easiest way to determine which case of weather you are trying to describe is just to memorize each individual type of weather vocabulary as a phrase:

"*Hace*" is usually used to express the general "feeling" of the weather (like it's hot, or cold, or foggy), "*hay*" and "*está*" are generally used to describe more specific types of weather.

To end this lesson, we will see some pretty colorful expressions in Spanish concerning the weather. These two are used when it's raining really hard:

- "It's raining oceans!" "*¡Llueve a mares!*"
- "It's raining pitchers / buckets!" "*¡Llueve a cántaros!*"

If it's been raining for days and you've had enough (or if someone is having a hard time in life), this rain-phrase means "this too shall pass":

- "Whenever it rained, it stopped." "*Siempre que llovió, paró.*"

These are couple of phrases that you may want to use when it's really cold:

- "It's so cold it burns your skin!" "*Hace un frío que pela.*"
- "I'm freezing!" "*¡Me estoy congelando!*"

And this one is used when it's a little warmer:

- "It's an oven." "*¡Es un horno!*"

CHAPTER 14:

GETTING DIRECTIONS

Getting directions can be very important. If you have a personal GPS, you might not need to ask but you never know when you might need to ask a stranger which way to go. Maybe you have lost your way or you could be visiting a different town and just need some advice.

If you're in a new town and you're looking to do some sightseeing, you can say "where" (which means "dónde") to ask where to go. But, you will also know when to use the verb "*estar*" and when to use the verb "*haber*", so you can ask "where is it?" :Where is it" can be both "*¿dónde está?*" and "*¿dónde hay?*".

Since they're used in slightly different situations, let's see an example of its use:

- "Where is Milo's tavern?" "*¿Dónde <u>está</u> la taberna de Milo?*
- "Where is there a doctor?" "*¿Dónde <u>hay</u> un doctor?*"

In the first example you're looking for a specific place (Milo's tavern). In the second example you're looking for a doctor, any doctor will do. You can tell this because in the first example we've used the definite article "*la*" (the), while the second sentence uses the indefinite article "*un*" (a).

To summarise, you'll use "*¿Dónde está...?*" any time you'd normally say "Where is the...?", and you'll use "*¿Dónde hay...?*" when you'd say "Where is a...?". (Another easy way to remember it is that you use "*está*" with definite articles (i.e., "the") and "*hay*" with indefinite articles (i.e., "a", "an").

More examples:

- "Where is the Garcia's house?" "¿Dónde está la casa de los García?"
- "Where is Juan and Leonardo's school? (Literally: "Where is the school of Juan and Leonardo?)"" "¿Dónde está la escuela de Juan y Leonardo?"
- "Where is a book store?" "¿Dónde hay una librería?"
- "Where is an ATM?" "¿Dónde hay un cajero automático?"

Once you've got your está and your hay situation sorted, here are some of the responses you might hear in Spanish:

"Across from…" "En frente de…"
"Next to…" "Al lado de…"
"Behind…" "Detrás de…"
"Between… and…." "Entre… y…"
"On…" "En…"

Examples:

1. "Next to the gas station." "Al lado de la gasolinera."
2. "Between the pharmacy and the school." "Entre la farmacia y la escuela."
3. "On the corner." "En la esquina."

But you might also hear:

"Two blocks (from here)." "A dos cuadras."
"Ten minutes (from here)." "A diez minutos."
"It's the next one." "Es la próxima."

Sometimes people might need to give you more specific directions, so they could say to "walk three blocks", "turn left", or "continue on for 15 minutes...":

- "Turn left" can be said in this form "dobla a la izquierda" or this other "gira a la izquierda". And the same goes with "turn right" which can be said in this form "dobla a la derecha" or this other "gira a la derecha".
- "Cross…" "Cruza..."
- "Continue…" "Sigue…"

- "Go straight ahead." *"Sigue derecho."*

Lastly, if you ask "Is it far?", *"¿Está lejos?"*, and the answer is "*sí*", then you might need to use the public transport system. Here is some vocabulary:

- "Take…" *"Toma…"*
- "… the bus." *"… el autobús."*
- "… the subway" *"… el metro"*
- "… the train" *"… el tren"*
- "… a taxi" *"… un taxi"*

Let's have a look at how to write addresses in Spanish. Address structures change according to countries and regions. Latin America and Spain do it slightly differently than in the USA and other parts of the world.

In this lesson we will look at cover format, abbreviations, and special terms that are helpful if you wish to write a letter, send a package, or you're planning an upcoming trip to a Spanish-speaking country.

The address format used in Hispanic countries goes from specific to general with one exception. In the U.S., the street number is first, in Latin America and Spain the street name goes first, before the number. Then you add the name of the *"colonia"* or *"vecindario"* ("neighborhood") and *"municipio"* ("municipality"). At the end goes the *"código postal"* ("zip code") which is the most important part.

See this example of how to write an address in Spanish:

- Simon Bolivar #37
  Colonia Agualongo
  Municipio de Santo Fernando
  Tolimá, Colombia
  Código Postal 02617

Street types are named based on length, width, number of roads, number of lanes, and even purpose. The abbreviation is usually included in an address. So let's take a look at some examples of street types that you will find in Latin America:

- *"Las avenidas"* ("the avenues") have wide sidewalks and trees. They are the most common streets; they usually have stores, cafes, and other places where people can meet up or shop. The abbreviation in English is "Ave." and in Spanish, is "*Av.*"
- *"Los bulevares"* ("the boulevards") are wide streets with tall landscaping. Its urban and cultural importance is above avenidas and regular streets.
- *"Las carreteras"* ("the highways") are roads that connect towns or cities. These streets are designed for high speed vehicles and are not safe for pedestrians.
- *"Las cerradas"* ("the dead-end-streets") are streets that end in a dead end (they lead nowhere). The abbreviation in Spanish is "*Cda.*"
- *"Las calles de un solo sentido"* ("one-way streets") these are made for low-speed, semi-local traffic. Traffic calming measures can be taken in order to achieve those purposes.
- *"Las calles de doble sentido"* ("two-way streets") are wider streets with heavier traffic than the one-way streets.
- *"Los callejones"* ("alleys") are narrow streets that can be pedestrian-only or one-way streets for small cars.
- *"Las calles peatonales"* ("pedestrian streets") are streets made exclusively for pedestrians. Only cultural or commercial districts offer these spaces for shoppers and tourists.

Stores, offices, and restaurants use more specific land markers so you might want to include those as well. So if the hotel, bank, or museum has a confusing address, adding in a landmark description will help the delivery person or yourself. If you want to practice writing an address in Spanish, remember that all references can be included.

The following example includes street type, "*calle*" ("street"), "*edificio*" ("building"), "*piso*" ("floor"), "*departamento*" ("apartment"), and adjacent streets.

- Calle de Simon Bolivar #37
  Edificio Márquez
  Piso 4 – Departmento 16

Colonia Agualongo
Entre calles Bernal y Santiago
Municipio de Santo Fernando
Tolimá, Colombia
Código Postal 02617

"Entre calles" means "between streets" and it is used when the place in question is in the middle of the block. So if the location is in a corner, you can say *"esquina con..."* ("corner with") and the name of the other street.

CHAPTER 15:

TRAVELING IN SPANISH SPEAKING COUNTRIES

Since travel or *"viajar"* is one of the main reasons why people learn new languages, this is a vocabulary you may be interested in. If you're planning on visiting a Spanish-speaking country, you will need to know these words and phrases to help you get where you want to go.

Chances are you will likely have to take a plane, so let's look at some useful airport vocabulary:

"The arrivals." *"La llegadas."*
"The departures." *"Las partidas."*
"The terminal." *"La terminal."*
"The curstoms." *"La aduana."*
"The runway." *"La pista."*
"The layover." *"La escala."*
"The passport." *"El pasaporte."*
"The flight." *"El vuelo."*
"The luggage." *"El equipaje."*
"The ticket." *"El pasaje."*
"To take off." *"El despegar."*
"To land." *"Aterrizar."*

Now, if you have already reached your destination, you will probably use public transportation to get to where you want to go. To do that, you will need to incorporate the following vocabulary:

"The stop." "*La parada.*"

"The driver." "*El conductor.*"

"The destination." "*El destino.*"

"The transfer." "*El transbordo.*"

"Pay for the ticket." "*Pagar el boleto.*"

"Get on the bus." "*Subir al autobús.*"

"Get off the bus." "*Bajar del autobús.*"

Now we will see some useful phrases:

- "How can I get to...?" "*¿Cómo puedo ir a...?*"
- "Where does the bus / train to (Madrid) leave from?" "*¿De dónde sale el autobús/tren para (Madrid)?*"
- "At what time does the ferry leave to Ibiza?" "*¿A que hora sale el ferry a Ibiza?*"
- "Does this bus stop in (Córdoba)?" "*¿Este autobús para en (Córdoba)?*"
- "One ticket, please." "*Un boleto, por favor.*"
- "I get off at the next stop." "*Me bajo en la próxima parada.*"
- "Can you call a taxi for me?" "*¿Me puede llamar un taxi?*"
- "Is this taxi free (available)?" "*¿Este taxi está libre*"
- "I want to go to..." "*Quiero ir a...*"

But the traveling world doesn't end at the airport, before arriving or once the destination is reached, other useful words are:

- "The suitcase (or "bag")." "*La maleta.*"

  Used in the singular form, it means "suitcase." Each individual bag you have is a maleta.

  Used in the plural form, you can translate it as "luggage" or "*equipaje.*"

- "The passport." "*El pasaporte.*"

- "The tourist." "El turista", "La turista."

  Remember that nouns ending in -ista do not have a different feminine form. Male and female tourists are both called turistas. Only the article changes.

- "The souvenir." "*El recuerdo.*"

  "*Recuerdo*" comes from the verb "*recordar*", which means "to remember". Note: a memory is also called a "*recuerdo*" in Spanish!

- "The photo camera." "*La cámara de fotos.*"
- "The hotel." "*El hotel.*"

Let's see some examples of its use:

- "The flight was good; I met a cool tourist and took a picture of us with my camera." "*El vuelo estuvo bien; conocí a un turista genial y nos tomé una foto con mi cámara.*"
- "I went to get my luggage but one of my bags has been lost." "*Fui a buscar mi equipaje pero se ha perdido una de mis maletas.*"
- "I traveled to Spain and I bought a souvenir for my best friend." "*Viajé a España y compré un recuerdo para mi mejor amigo.*"
- "I'd like to buy a ticket for the next flight to Colombia, please." "*Me gustaría comprar un boleto para el próximo vuelo a Colombia, por favor.*"
- "We are looking for our stop at the terminal." "*Estamos buscando nuestra parada en la terminal.*"

In the following list you will find some countries ("*países*" in Spanish) and their respective nationalities, so that you can look them up quickly and easily.

Country	"País"	Nationality	Languaje
Spain	*España*	*Español*	*Español*
Brazil	*Brasil*	*Brasilero*	*Portugués*
Argentina	*Argentina*	*Argentino*	*Español*
Chile	*Chile*	*Chileno*	*Español*
Colombia	*Colombia*	*Colombiano*	*Español*
France	*Francia*	*Francés*	*Francés*
United States	*Estados Unidos*	*Estadounidense*	*Inglés*
Mexico	*México*	*Mexicano*	*Español*
England	*Inglaterra*	*Inglés*	*Inglés*
Italy	*Italia*	*Italiano*	*Italiano*
Japan	*Japón*	*Japonés*	*Japonés*
Canada	*Canadá*	*Canadiense*	*Inglés*

About nationalities:

In case the person uses a feminine pronoun, the final -o of the nationality is replaced (such as "*la brasilera*"). In words that end in a consonant, to obtain their feminine form, a final -*a* is added (like "*la española*"). As for words ending with -e, only the pronoun is modified, while the word remains the same (for example: "*la canadiense*").

- "Camila is Japanese and speaks Japanese." "*Camila es japonesa y habla japonés.*"
- "Jorge comes from Spain and speaks Spanish and Italian." "*Jorge viene de España y habla español e italiano.*"
- "I'm from France but I moved to Canada two years ago. Now I speak French and English." "*Soy de Francia pero me mudé a Canadá hace dos años. Ahora hablo francés e inglés.*"
- "My family is from Brazil and we all speak Portuguese." "*Mi familia es de Brasil y todos hablamos portugués.*"

CONCULSION

Farewell!

Congratulations on reaching the end of this book! It has been a pleasure to accompany you on this journey.

Now that you have seen how to introduce yourself, formulate sentences and basic vocabulary, you are ready to discuss your opinions and enjoy tourism in Spanish-speaking countries!

However, all this does not end here because you never finish learning a language, but you just get used to using it. That's the incredible thing about learning a language is that there are always new words or expressions to learn.

So here are three tips that you should keep in mind to continue improving your language skills:

- To make your pronunciation resemble that of a native speaker, it is essential to know the characteristic sounds of a language and not just its words or grammatical structure. Therefore, having an interaction with these speakers will be of great help.
- There is a general idea that if you do not travel to the country of the source language you cannot learn the language correctly, but this is only true when you are trying to reach an expert or native level. The important thing is the immersion that one has within the culture of that language, and thanks to the internet and the audiovisual resources available, it is not necessary to leave home to achieve it.

- As in any other language, it is enough to know a small percentage of the vocabulary to be able to communicate in most everyday situations. That is why instead of struggling to learn hundreds and hundreds of words, it is better to focus on the ones that are used the most at first.

Now it is time to say goodbye! I wish you a lot of success in your Spanish learning

Notes

Notes

Notes

Notes

Notes

www.ingramcontent.com/pod-product-compliance
Lightning Source LLC
Chambersburg PA
CBHW081113080526
44587CB00021B/3578